ACTIVITY IN MARX'S PHILOSOPHY

ACTIVITY IN MARX'S PHILOSOPHY

by

Norman D. Livergood

MARTINUS NIJHOFF / THE HAGUE / 1967

PRINTED IN THE NETHERLANDS

TO DAVID

INTRODUCTION

This essay attempts to demonstrate the significance of the principle of activity in the philosophy of Karl Marx. The principle of activity in Marx has both a general and a specific meaning. In general the principle refers to the activist element in Marxian *practice* motivating both Marx and his contemporary devotees. The specific facet of the principle relates to Marx's *philosophy* – the principle of activity being that concept which underlies the entire system.

Activity for Marx is both a philosophic concept and an element of human experience demanded by his system. Marx, that is, not only theorizes about activity but also illustrates his theory in his life. Hence, we find the principle of activity both in his writings and in his doings. Marx most often used the words *Action, Tätigkeit,* or *Praxis* to refer to the principle of activity.

No major philosopher has fully dealt with the concept of action. We sometimes suppose that action only occurs when we can observe some outward result or motion. Spinoza's definition of action disallows this narrow interpretation of activity.

> I say that we act when anything is done, either within us or without us, of which we are the adequate cause, that is to say ... when from our nature anything follows, either within us or without, which by that nature alone can be clearly and distinctly understood.[1]

The important point in Spinoza's definition is his contention that action is both an inward and an outward phenomenon: activity includes both thought and action. Hegel also defined activity as both active and non-active. For example, Hegel defined will as "mere doing which does nothing." [2] Later we shall see how Marx develops this same idea of the two aspects of activity.

[1] B. Spinoza, *Ethics.* (New York: Hafner, 1949), p. 128.
[2] G. W. F. Hegel, *The Phenomenology of Mind.* (London: Allen and Unwin, 1955), p. 432.

With Marx philosophy descended from the cloudy towers of mere speculation to the arena of practice. Certainly Hegel's transformation of traditional logic into material logic marked the first step in the direction of unifying theory and practice since it protested against the divorce of truth and reality. But Marx's system represents the full development of philosophy as *practical.* He first began to develop this idea in his doctoral dissertation, The Difference Between the Democritean and Epicurean Philosophy of Nature.

The dissertation shows Marx dissatisfied with the semi-action of the contemporary political intellectuals. He demands a transition from speculative philosophy to a "radical" critique which can be no less than an embodiment of the idea in reality through revolutionary action.[1]

Marx's dissertation traces the movement of the theoretical mind which has moved away from mundane reality after being transformed into an active entity in itself. In this, he says, there has arisen a conflict between the theoretical mind and worldly reality. Marx thought that philosophy could pass beyond the theoretical declarations of the seventeenth century only if the Aristotelian dichotomy between speculative and practical reason was corrected by revealing to man that he can be creative both through theory and practice – that the world is of his making and not something separated from him as reality from thought.

In the dissertation Marx is still a philosopher in the Hegelian style. He deals with such erudite concepts as: self-consciousness, necessity, pure particularity, abstract particularity, and declination of atoms. The foreword to the dissertation mentions Marx's intention to treat the whole of the Epicurean, Stoic and Sceptical systems. The dissertation was to be merely a prelude to the more extensive treatment. Marx, however, never wrote the larger work, and the dissertation deals primarily with Epicurus, treating Democritus in contrast.

We cannot be sure of Marx's motives in attempting to deal with these early philosophic systems. Mehring points out that the early concept of self-consciousness could be related to Marx's later idea of the necessity of the self-consciousness of the proletarian class. A class, Marx was later to say, becomes self-conscious when it awakens to its interests as these conflict with other class interests.

Each of the members of the philosophical Montagne (as Ruge called Marx, Bauer and Köppen) dealt with the Epicurean, Stoic and Scep-

[1] E. Voegelin, "The Formation of the Marxian Revolutionary Idea," *Review of Politics*, 12, 1950, p. 278.

tical systems. In his work on King Frederick, Köppen, for example, shows how this classic figure of the Enlightenment assimilated the ideas of Epicureanism, Stoicism and Scepticism into his life. They became, Köppen says, the essential facets of his intellectual and aesthetic existence. Bruno Bauer "studied Stoicism, Epicureanism, and Scepticism to clarify the origins of Christianity which led him to a criticism of the Gospels, of which the profundity and audacity went well beyond Strauss and dealt even harsher blows to orthodoxy." [1]

Within these philosophical schools Marx chose to work with the natural philosophies of Democritus and Epicurus. Marx sharply differentiates between Democritus and Epicurus. Earlier scholars, from Cicero to Leibniz, considered Epicurus only a poor copy of Democritus. After Marx, Zeller was to prove this "copy" theory incorrect. But Marx predates Zeller's argument and in his dissertation seizes on the contrast between the two Greek philosophers.

It is in Epicurus' concept of the declination of the atoms that Marx finds the most fruitful grounds for the development of his own thought. The atom with its activity of declination became a symbol of the active self for Marx. Whereas Democritus had remained in the realm of external determinism, Epicurus offers a more fruitful conception of *self*-determination. If the atom can be viewed as inwardly active, then we can escape mechanistic determinism.

Throughout the dissertation this "animating principle" of Epicurus assumes great importance for Marx. In fact, as Mehring says, it was this concept of activity which was to preclude Marx's completion of the projected work on the philosophy of self-consciousness. Marx could no longer remain in the realm of purely theoretical philosophy; his philosophy became the active theorizing leading to the transformation of the world.

In his doctoral thesis we find Marx condemning the other students of Hegel for a too slavish acceptance of the master. For though Marx is still a Hegelian in the dissertation, he dares to challenge Hegel and attempts to go beyond him.

In one of his early works Marx explicitly states that the subject of his dissertation was suggested by the awareness of the parallel between post-Aristotelian and post-Hegelian philosophy. After both these philosophic giants had constructed their enormous systems, it remained the task of philosophy to realize, to make *practical*, the ideas of the masters.

[1] F. Mehring, "La Thèse de Karl Marx sur Démocrite et Epicure," *La Nouvelle Critique*, 61, Janvier 1955, p. 5 (translated by the author).

Marx saw his mission as the transposition into practice of the whole order of things which Aristotle and Hegel had reserved to the theoretical intellect. The theoretical, as opposed to the practical mind, when free (as after Aristotle and Hegel), is transformed into practical energy and turns to act upon material reality. Just as the post-Aristotelian period had emphasized practical, ethical self-determination, so Marx desires to rescue man from the post-Hegelian impasse by reclaiming the world in practice (not in pure theory as he thought Hegel had done).

Taking the principle of activity as first developed in Marx's dissertation, I shall show how it influences his materialism, his epistemology, and his conception of philosophy. Because of the importance of Marx's dissertation, I have translated it from the original German into English. This is the first complete English translation of the dissertation, though portions of it have been translated earlier by McCoy, Mins, and Voegelin. The translation appears as an appendix to this essay.

In tracing the concept of activity in Marx's philosophy, this study will give primary emphasis to his early writings. It is in these that the concept finds its genesis and development. Marx's later works are a consistent outgrowth of this and other germinal concepts.

> In broad outline, what Marx expressed in the early writing is the essence of Marxism as it was to remain and develop through the remaining thirty-nine years of his life.[1]

[1] R. Dunayevskaya, *Marxism and Freedom.* (New York: Bookman Associates, 1958), p. 64

CONTENTS

AN ENGLISH TRANSLATION OF MARX'S DOCTORAL DISSERTATION

THE DIFFERENCE BETWEEN THE DEMOCRITEAN AND EPICUREAN PHILOSOPHY OF NATURE

CHAPTER I

ACTIVITY AND MATERIALISM

"Life is not determined by consciousness, but consciousness by life."

(Marx: *German Ideology*)

I. INTRODUCTION

Within Marx's own peculiar kind of materialism, dialectical materialism, the concept of activity plays a most important role. It is the idea of activity which sets Marx's materialism apart from other types. This principle of activity distinguishes Marx's materialism from idealism – for Marx incorporated some of the fundamental notions of idealism in his materialism. Marx's materialism is made dialectical by the presence of activity within it.

Marx's materialism stands as one of the most original and distinctive facets of his entire philosophy. It was this aspect of his thought about which Engels chose to speak at Marx's grave.

Just as Darwin discovered the law of evolution in organic nature, so Marx discovered the law of evolution in human history; he discovered the simple fact, hitherto concealed by an overgrowth of ideology, that mankind must first of all eat and drink, have shelter and clothing, before it can pursue politics, religion, science, art, etc. ... and that therefore the production of the immediate material means of subsistence and consequently the degree of economic development attained by a given people or during a given epoch, form the foundation upon which the state institutions, the legal conceptions, the art and even the religious ideas of the people concerned have been evolved, and in the light of which these things must be explained, in stead of vice versa as had hitherto been the case.[1]

2. MARX AND OLD MATERIALISM

Marx was interested in materialism even as early as the writing of his doctoral dissertation. In the dissertation he is still writing as a Young-Hegelian. He chooses Epicurus' atomism over that of Democritus for in the former he finds the necessary idea of activity. It is the concept of free activity which Marx considers Epicurus' most significant contribution to materialism.

[1] V. Venable, *Human Nature: The Marxian View.* (New York: A. A. Knopf, 1945), p. 29.

Democritus concerned himself exclusively with the material existence of the atom, whereas Epicurus concerned himself further with the atom as a conception, with its form as well as its matter, with its essence as well as its existence. Epicurus regarded the atom as being not only the material basis of the world of phenomena, but also the symbol of the isolated individual, the formal principle of abstract individual self-consciousness. [1]

In *The Holy Family*, Marx discusses materialism, especially the materialism of the eighteenth century. Perhaps the thing which bothered Marx the most about the materialism of the past was its attempt to explain all things mechanistically. Such mechanism was necessary because nothing was allowed to exist but atoms in a void acting *externally* upon one another.

If the infinite fall of atoms were to be the explanation of all natural events, then Marx could see that mechanism would be the basic law of nature. All motion would be mechanical, i.e. change in place as the result of external action. To Marx this was no explanation at all; it provided man no understanding of nature's ways.

So began Marx's search for a non-mechanistic explanation of natural events. He found the hint of a solution in some of the eighteenth century materialists. Holbach had realized the necessity of a non-mechanistic definition of matter.

If we understand by nature a mass of dead, qualityless, completely passive bodies, then of course we shall be compelled to look for the principle of its movement outside of that nature. But if we understand by nature what in fact it really is, a whole whose different parts have different qualities, which henceforth act in accordance with these different qualities, being in constant action and reaction one upon the other, which possess weight, gravitate to a common centre, whilst others go away from it, and move to the circumference, which muturally attract and repel one another, are united and divided, and which by their continual clashes and drawing together again produce and decompose all the bodies visible to us, then we are not compelled to have recourse to supernatural forces in order to explain to ourselves the formation of things and of visible phenomena. [2]

Condorcet was able to see a progressive movement of human society through stages whose development followed definite laws. Also (and this was to prove significant to Marx's economic theory), Condorcet correlated these laws of development with corresponding advances of production technique. Diderot posited the inseparability of matter from motion, and though never in a definite way, he gave intimations of a principle of activity in atoms.

1 F. Mehring, *Karl Marx.* (Ann Arbor: University of Michigan Press, 1962), p. 29.
2 G.V. Plekhanov,*Essays in the History of Materiolism.* (London: J. Lane, 1934), pp. 5, 6.

A body in itself, by the nature of its essential qualities, is full of action and of energy, whether one considers it molecule by molecule or whether one considers it in the mass.

. . . .

Force which acts on the molecule exhausts itself; force which is a part of the molecule does not exhaust itself. It is immutable, eternal. [1]

In each of these materialists – Holbach, Condorcet, Diderot – there was the concept of the *internal* movement of material elements. It was this idea which was to find more comprehensive development in Marx's materialism.

3. IDEALISM AS THE BASIS OF MARX'S MATERIALISM

Marx found the solution to the classical problem of materialism (how action can be explained in non-mechanistic terms) in idealism.

Marx did not reject idealism. "Thoroughgoing Naturalism or Humanism," as the young Marx designated his own philosophic outlook, "distinguishes itself from idealism and from materialism and is at the same time the truth uniting both." Marxism may be said to be the most idealistic of all materialistic philosophy, and Hegelianism the most materialistic of all idealistic philosophy.[2]

It was the principle of dialectical activity which proved to be the answer for Marx. It was from Hegel's dialectical principle that Marx drew most heavily. Dialectics, Marx saw, posits the inseparability of matter and motion. Motion, in fact, *is* the mode of existence of matter. The mechanistic view had seen reality as composed of ready-made things, each with its own fixed properties. Dialectics saw the world as a complex of processes in which all things arise, have their existence and pass away.

In fact, all the existing forms of materialism were unacceptable to Marx because they lacked a vitalizing principle. They regarded matter as inert, and Marx did not believe that it was such. They regarded mechanical motion as the only form of motion, while Marx believed that there were other and more important forms of motion.[3]

In Epicurus Marx discovered an idea capable of transforming materiialism into a complete system of thought – a system able to explain change in non-mechanistic terms. Epicurus' concept of the declination of atoms was the beginning of the idea of an internal principle of

[1] M. Cornforth, *In Defense of Philosophy.* (New York: International Publishers, 1950), p. 43.

[2] R. Dunayevskaja, *op. cit.*, p. 42.

[3] C. J. McFadden, *The Philosophy of Communism.* (New York: Benziger Brothers, 1939), p. 27.

motion within reality. But the thought was not fully developed – always remained a foreshadowing. It was in Hegel that this notion burst into full expression.

Reality, Hegel affirmed, has within it the principle of self-movement. An entity maintains itself by overcoming and incorporating the manifold of external elements it experiences and bringing all opposing elements into an internal harmony. The being of a thing is the entire dynamic of its becoming something else and unifying itself with its other. Something can be known only by knowing its development – its history. It is this movement or force which constitutes the reality of an entity. But the movement is not arbitrary, it operates according to principles – *dialectical* principles.

It was Feuerbach who first gave Marx the idea of using Hegel's idealism as the basis for his own materialism.

> Feuerbach, though unsatisfactory in his crude materialism, gave to Marx and Engels an invaluable clue to the solution of their problem. In his attempted presentation of a new materialism, he had utilized, to some extent, the dialectic of Hegel. Marx and Engels were not slow to see the possibilities of this procedure. They suddenly saw that in idealism was to be found the very elements upon which there could be erected a living, vitalized philosophy of materialism. The dialectic had been the heart and soul of Hegel's idealism – they would make it the heart and soul of their materialism.[1]

Feuerbach had transformed Hegel's idea of the self-alienation of the Idea into the concept of the self-alienation of man in the unconscious projection of man's needs into religious objects and ideas. For Feuerbach, objects of worship are hypostatizations of human desire. Man, finding his existence barren and unrewarding, constructs a heaven peopled with anthropomorphic beings and objects.

Feuerbach had correctly interpreted religious and philosophic phenomena as the projection and reification of elements of human desire into objects of worship or theories.

But Feuerbach's theories remained too much on the level of abstraction for Marx. He was able to explain how man projected an imaginary realm of religion and philosophy in answer to his unrealized needs. But Feuerbach, Marx said, had not been able to see the most important issue; there must be a reason *why* the mundane man fixes for himself an independent realm in the clouds.

Marx thought Feuerbach had to some extent avoided what he called Hegel's mystifications by making man the basis of his system. But

[1] C. J. McFadden, *ibid.*, p. 28.

Feuerbach, Marx asserted, did not go far enough. In place of Feuerbach's absolute man, Marx, substituted social man. In the *German Ideologie* Marx says of Feuerbach:

> But apart from the fact that he only conceives him as a "sensuous object," not as "sensuous activity," because he still remains in the realm of theory and conceives of men not in their given social connection, not under their existing conditions of life, which have made them what they are, he never arrives at the really existing active men, but stops at the abstraction "man," and gets no further than recognizing "the True, individual, corporeal man" emotionally, i.e. he knows no other "human relationships" of man to man" than love and friendship, and even then idealized. He gives no criticism of the present conditions of life. Thus he never manages to conceive the sensuous world as the total living sensuous activity of the individuals composing it; and therefore when, for example, he sees instead of healthy men a crowd of scrofulous, over-worked and consumptive starvelings, he is compelled to take refuge in the "higher perception" and in the ideal "compensation in the species," and thus to relapse into idealism at the very point where the communist materialist sees the necessity, and at the same time the condition, of a transformation both of industry and of the social structure.[1]

Taking his impulse from Feuerbach, Marx set out to develop a new materialism incorporating within it some of the principles of Hegelian idealism.

4. MARX'S CRITICISM OF HEGEL

Though Marx borrowed heavily from Hegel, he did so in such a way that he thought he had completely transformed Hegel's thought. Marx felt that Hegel was wrong in seeing thought as the source of dialectical principles; from pure theorizing Hegel thought he had gained wisdom. On the contrary, Marx held Hegel's dialectical principles were abstracted from facts. It is in material reality, not thought, that dialectical laws evolve and are discovered. If Marx relied on Hegel for the form of the dialectic, this, he maintained, was because he was certain, whether Hegel admitted it or not, that the laws had been derived from the world, from the practical interconnections of human existence. Marx firmly maintained that "the real truths in Hegel are not the outcome of his philosophical principles, but are as it were smuggled in as the result of his wide empirical knowledge and his reflections on it." [2]

Dialectical principles are to be derived from empirical actualities and factual generalizations, Marx said. In Hegel the dialectical move-

[1] K. Marx, *The German Ideology*. (New York: International Publishers, 1939), p. 37.
[2] H. P. Adams, *Karl Marx in his Earlier Writings*. (London: Allen and Unwin, 1940), p. 74.

ment had started from the abstract nature of being and man. Marx considered his own operation to be, in contradistinction, the avoidance of metaphysics which to him was nothing but irresponsible speculation and the reification of concepts.

Marx believed that in Hegel the dialectic stood on its head. For Hegel the self-development of thought is the real movement and facts are only reflections of this superior reality. Actually, said Marx, the dialectical movement is merely a reflection of the actual development of the real world. So Marx sets out to put the dialectic back on its feet. Dialectical laws, he maintains, are abstracted from facts.

In the view of Marx, social, political and religious ideas are not primary; they are merely reflections of the underlying reality – material conditions.

In the social production which men carry on they enter into definite relations that are indispensable and independent of their will; these relations of production correspond to a definite stage of development of their material powers of production. The sum total of these relations of production constitutes the economic construction of society – the real foundation on which rise legal and political superstructures and to which correspond definite forms of social consciousness. The mode of production in material life determines the general character of the social, political and spiritual processes of life. It is not the consciousness of men that determines their existence, but, on the contrary, their social existence determines their consciousness.[1]

What Marx accepted in Hegel was his emphasis on the active side of man's nature. But Hegel had conceived of this as purely theoretical, not real, sensuous activity as such, Marx thought. Hegel's whole system is one of concepts; the universal idea is taken as the subject, real concrete entities as predicates. Actuality as a predicate is dealt with as a mere determination of the idea. Marx contended that Hegel had seen the problems of the world as problems of idea, thus Hegel's solution was posited in the realm of the pure intellect. Problems are solved by means of theoretical pronouncements and systems of thought. Marx struggled fiercely against this by means of his own criticism.

Speculatieve philosophy, to be exact, *Hegel's* philosophy, must transpose all questions from the form of human common sense to the form of speculative reason and change the real question into a *speculative* one to be able to answer it.[2]

[1] K. Marx, *A Contribution to the Critique of Political Economy.* (New York: International Publishers, 1904), p. 11.

[2] K. Marx, *The Holy Family.* (Moscow: Foreign Languages Publishing House, 1956), p. 111. (hereafter cited as *HF*).

Marx accepted the form of the dialectic from Hegel but changed its content. For Marx, the dialectic is a matter of social relation. The moments of opposition are objective conditions independent of thought. The opposing elements are classes; moments of opposition become revolutionary phases of development.

Marx's rejection of Hegel's idealism does not take into consideration many of the subleties of Hegel's thought. Marx's broadsides ignore the fine shadings of Hegel's theory. He interprets Hegel in a very general way and then sets his own views over against this. Even the language of Marx's criticism of Hegel lacks precision. What, for example, does Marx mean by saying that in Hegel the dialectic stands on its head? He appears to say that in Hegel thought is the prior reality, sensuous existence is subsidiary. This, as an interpretation of Hegel's thought, is surely not entirely correct. For Hegel goes to great pains to avoid such a simplistic interpretation of his philosophy.

Marx's lack of precision in criticizing Hegel can be seen, for example, in *Capital* where he claims that for Hegel the real "is only the outward manifestation of the idea."

5. MARX AND THE YOUNG-HEGELIANS

Marx leveled the same charge of abstraction and mere theorizing at his immediate contemporaries, the Young-Hegelians. Followers of Hegel had split into two divisions: 1) Hegelians of the Right, who emphasized Hegel's reactionary side, and 2) Hegelians of the Left, who emphasized Hegel's ideas of change and development. It was in struggling with and against these Hegelians of the Left (as Hook has pointed out) that Marx came to the full development of his thought.

Marx himself began as a Young-Hegelian. He was attracted to Hegel's idealism because he wished to unite thought and reality. He was closely associated with most of the Young-Hegelians at one time or another: Meyen, Rutenberg, Herwegh, the three Bauers, Strauss, Ruge, Jung, Oppenheim, Feuerbach, and others.

Though these men were his friends and colleagues, he found their views at variance with his own and did not hesitate to criticize them. The majority of his early works are written in answer and in opposition to these Young-Hegelians.

All Hegelians of the Left had begun their intellectual careers by attacking the religion of their day.

We have heard so much of Marx's atheism that it seems almost natural to relate him to this phase of Hegelianism of the Left. But Marx's atheism, like his other views, was something he worked out in the course of his intellectual development; he did not accept atheism ready-made. In fact, in early life Marx had been at least a nominal Christian. Though coming from a Jewish background, the young Marx had been introduced to Christianity when his father espoused Protestanism for business and social reasons. In his early academic career Marx had been a moral idealist and had even written an essay on union with Christ!

One of the most scathing attacks on religion in that day was F. David Strauss' *Leben Jesu.* In this work Strauss attempted to show that the gospels were so inherently contradictory that one could in no way accept them as historically accurate. The early Christians, reared in the tradition of the Old Testament, had constructed the gospel accounts. The New Testament record of the life and work of Jesus was no more than the creation of the myth-making consciousness of the early Christian community.

The value of Christianity for Strauss was that it had conceived of the unity of God and man, thus overcoming metaphysical dualism. But whereas Christianity had restricted such unity of deity and humanity to the person of Jesus, Strauss advocated that the whole human species must become the exemplification of the Man-god.

Strauss' book caused a furor, even among his associates. Bruno Bauer attacked the book openly and was thus thought by some to be orthodox. Bauer was especially well-liked by the Minister of Culture, Altenstein. But in 1839 Bauer showed his heresy when he argued with a professor named Hengstenberg. Altenstein, wishing to save Bauer from government attack, sent him to Bonn as a lecturer, with hopes of appointing him to a professorship.

But then the final blow was struck; Bauer wrote his own criticism of the gospels, *Kritik der evangelischen Geschichte der Synoptiker,* which proved him to be even more heretical than Strauss. He rejected Strauss' idea of an unconscious mythical creation of the gospels. According to their several purposes, the individual evangelists had created the Messianic figure of Jesus. On the basis of careful analysis and biblical criticism, he denied not only the divinity of Jesus but also his historicity.

Marx himself maintained that the religious problem arises from the social and not vice versa as Bauer held. Religious difficulties, Marx wrote, will be overcome when their social basis is dissolved. Marx insisted that religion comes not from symbolic patchwork (Strauss) or from the ideas of leaders (Bauer) but from the inverted expression of natural and social desires (Feuerbach).

Much of Marx's writing is witty and stylistically pleasing, and especially is this the case in his attack on Bauer and other Young- Hegelians. He charged that Bauer had not been able to rid himself of the Holy Ghost – the Holy Ghost was still writing through Bauer in the form of "self-consiousness." Marx parodied the attempt of the Young-Hegelians to answer social problems by means of theory alone. Their effort he satirically called "Critical Criticism."

And therefore Criticism has so loved the mass that it sent its only begotten son, that all who believe in him may not be lost, but that they may have Critical lifc.[1]

Several of Marx's early books are given over entirely to attacking this Critical Criticism. The *Holy Family* was written in opposition to Bauer and others. This title has two implications. First, it is related to the sixth chapter of Feuerbach's *Das Wesen des Christenthums* where the "holy family" refers to needs of the early Christian community. Secondly, the title refers to the Bauer brothers.

Marx's purpose in these writings is to show the futility of speculative criticism. Such speculation, Marx maintained, deals with man in the abstract, as idea or spirit, not as concrete, sensuous man. Marx held that Critical Criticism was still religious in its tenor, for any theory was religious for him if it used transcendental terms which became reified. Bauer's atheism was a sham to Marx; Bauer continued to act and think in religious terms though espousing complete non-belief. But this was not real atheism for Marx.

Marx affirmed that for Critical Criticism reality is thought. The task of the critic is to trace out the lines of theoretical development. The basis of all social difficulty is to be found in ideas. The technique of the Critical Critic, Marx insisted, was mystification, confusion and abstraction. He attacked Szeliga for making mysteries out of real trivialities. "His art," Marx said, "is not that of disclosing what ishidden, but of hiding what is disclosed." By abstracting one element from others, reifying this, and making it primary, the Critical Critics arrive at monstrous distortions, Marx contended.

If from real apples, pears, strawberries and almonds I form the general idea "Fruit," if I go further and *imagine* that my abstract idea "Fruit," derived from

[1] K. Marx, *HF*. p. 17.

real fruit, is an entity existing outside me, is indeed the *true* essence of the pear, the apple, etc.; then, in the *language of speculative philosophy* I am declaring that "Fruit" is the *substance* of the pear, the apple, the almond, etc. I am saying, therefore, that to be a pear is not essential to the pear, that to be an apple is not essential to the apple, that what is essential to these things is not their real being, perceptible to the senses, but the essence I have abstracted from them and then foisted on them, the essence of my idea – "Fruit." I therefore declare apples,pears, almonds, etc., to be mere forms of existence, modi, of "Fruit." [1]

In these words Marx exposes what he considers to be the method of the speculative philosophers, The major defect of the abstractionism of the Young-Hegelians, says Marx, is that it does not contribute either to proper understanding or to realistic change. Taking concepts, ideas, notions as the basic reality, they consider that all one must do is transform theories and conditions will automatically improve. Since they consider ideas the real chains of men, they fight only against these illusions of the consciousness.

6. MARX'S DIALECTICAL MATERIALISM

It is in reaction to the Young-Hegelians that Marx creates his most scathing attack and at the same time his most original concepts. The real basis of human life is man's *activity*, he asserts. It is the action of man – his labor, his associations – which serves as a foundation for ideas and not vice versa. This is the keynote of Marx's materialism: "Life is not determined by consciousness, but consciousness by life." One must not begin with abstract ideas and hope to arrive at reality. Abstractions of any sort must be completely relinquished. Man's material activity is the foundation of his existence, not his theories. Marx points up the defect of his opponents and promulgates his own method of investigation in these words:

It has not occurred to any one of these philosophers to inquire into the connection of German philosophy with German reality, the relation of their critisicm to their own material surroundings.[2]

The premises from which we bigin are not arbitrary ones, not dogmas, but real premises from which abstraction can only be made in the imagination. They are the real individuals, their activity and the material conditions under which they live, both those which they find already existing and those produced by their activity.[3]

[1] K. Marx, *HF*, p. 78.

[2] K. Marx, *The German Ideology*. (New York: International Publishers, 1939), p. 15. (Hereafter cited as *GI*).

[3] *Ibid.*, pp. 6, 7.

Other philosophers and thinkers had placed emphasis on man's practical side – notably the French Materialists and British Empiricists. But none of these earlier men had placed the basis of their philosophy so close to man's everyday life. Marx asserted that what a man *does* each day – working, relating to others – is the primary fact of his existence.

Marx's mistake was in over-emphasizing one kind of activity to the exclusion of all others: economic activity. Some apologists of Marxism have rightly pointed out that in some passages Marx speaks of the material base of reality as being more inclusive than economic relations. But by and large such passages are not representative of his general thought. More and more Marx came to place greatest emphasis on economic relations – "means of production."

In some of the early writings, Marx's concept of activity included all human actions. Indeed, this is one of his original criticisms of private property. Private property, he said, brings about the denial of all other actions by the activity of owning. Marx desired that man be able to realize his full potential, so that every side of his life be developed. Communist society was to allow a man to do that work which he desired and which was at the same time best for society. In Marx's earlier view of communist society, activity included all of man's life – not merely his economic existence. Had Marx gone on to develop this more general view of man's activity he would have avoided making economic conditions the primary factor in human existence.

Marx's later view of activity in which he placed greatest emphasis on the economic aspect of man is in error as are all partial answers. To make economic relations the primary basis for all of human life is to distort and misinterpret. Such a theory stands as a needed contrast to excessive idealistic contentions that ideas are the prime movers of history. But man does not live by labor alone. Man works, yes, but he also does other things which are of equal importance.

Marxism would be a far more valuable philosophy today had Marx worked out the implications of his earlier concept of activity in regard to his materialism.

CHAPTER II

ACTIVITY AND KNOWLEDGE

The question whether human thought can achieve objective truth is not a question of theory but a practical question.
(*Theses on Feuerbach*)

I. INTRODUCTION

In this chapter we shall explore the bearing of the principle of activity on Marx's epistemology. As with other topics, Marx's epistemology is seldom explicitly set forth and must be discerned within the general context of his writings. Most of the discussion of this topic is restricted to his early works. One of the most explicit passages deality with epistemology is found in Marx's *Theses on Feuerbach.*

Marx's significance in regard to the theory of knowledge is implicit and indirect. We must not expect to find a full-blown discussion of this topic separate from other subjects. Though indirect and implied, Marx's influence on epistemology is nonetheless profound. We shall see that his most significant contribution here is in relation to the principle of activity.

Since the time of Descartes, epistemology has become one of the most important problems in philosophy. The Cartesian method of doubt has become the prevailing philosophic technique in epistemology. The initiate in philosophy cuts his teeth on the "Cogito" argument and learns to hold in abeyance all but the most certain of knowledge – self-knowledge.

Epistemology, has, in fact, been so extensively treated that at the present it seems to be experiencing a period of disrepute if not total rejection. The issues would appear to have become so well-fixed and the possible solutions so often rehearsed that an outcry is heard whenever the question of man's knowledge is raised in philosophic company.

2. MARX AND MATERIALISM

In earlier sections we have seen how Marx was influenced by materialism (e.g. Feuerbach's materialism). Such influence is equally marked in relation to his epistemological views. Marx saw the difficulty in which earlier materialism had become involved. If all is matter then ideas must somehow be identical with or related to matter. But this view creates problems. How can we explain perception in strict materialistic terms? Hobbes' doctrine of phantasms is only one attempt at explanation which failed. Other equally difficult problems present themselves.

> The very existence of ideas constituted a difficulty which it originally tried to answer by regarding ideas as a tenuous kind of matter, and later, as sense impressions of varying degrees of complexity resulting from the bombardment of material particles on sensitive nerve endings. ... The standard formula which was invoked, viz., that a true idea was one which "agreed" or "corresponded" with its object, raised problems just as baffling. The proper meaning of correspondence presupposed a qualitative identity between the entities corresponding with each other, as e.g., the correspondence between a yardstick and some other standard measure, or a picture and an original. But what could this common element be? Material? This would mean that ideas would be back to Hegel and the coherence theory of truth.[1]

These problems above are merely a few of the many difficulties facing the early materialist epistemology. Marx inherited this legacy of epistemological quandary. It was his desire to remain within the materialist framework while avoiding its difficulties with regard to human knowledge. His job was to develop a new form of materialism.

We have seen how Marx rejected reductionist materialism, i.e. that materialism which reduces everything (including ideas) to matter in space. Marx allowed for the reality of thought *and* ideas. Thought is integrally tied up with material objects and does not have completely separate reality. Thought is the reflection of matter which occurs in the mind. Ideas are constructed from man's contact with external reality. In Marx's own words:

> Our conception of history ... explains the formation of ideas from material practice.[2]

Such a conception of thought implies that knowledge is active at both its poles. Reality, which for Marx was material practice, is the activity of man which produces thought. The object (active being) itself creates ideas because of its own form and structure. And, on the other hand, man's mind is active in knowledge in that it abstracts from reality and constructs ideas in the process of working with reality. Knowledge, for Marx, is not the merely passive reception of ideas from

[1] S. Hook, *From Hegel to Marx*, (New York: John Day, 1940), pp. 282, 283.
[2] K. Marx, *GI*, p. 28.

objects; knowledge involves a necessary activity of the mind with the external world. Before investigating all the aspects of Marx's activist theory of knowledge we shall trace its origin.

3. MARX AND IDEALISM

In earlier sections of this book we have seen how Marx adopted idealist principles in revising materialism. Here again, in epistemology, Marx finds in idealism the very elements needed in the kind of materialism which would solve the earlier problems of knowledge.

Marx saw the beginning of a solution in Kant's idealism. Kant had ascribed certain innate functions to mind which it performed in coming to knowledge. His Copernican Revolution in epistemology is actually a promulgation of mind's necessary activity in knowledge. Whereas before philosophers had considered knowledge merely mind's *conformity* to objects, the Copernican Revolution means that now the mind is active and demands that objects conform to its functions. The mind thus stands "as an appointed judge who compels the witnesses to answer the questions which he himself proposes."

Kant disagreed with earlier epistemologists that knowledge is merely passive perception.

> Ordinary sense-perception is by no means, according to Kant, a merely passive reception of sensations, it involves a highly complex mental activity.[1]

The knowledge process, for Kant, involves a whole series of complex actions performed on the received manifold of sensations.

> The manifold of representations may be given in an intuition which is purely sensuous, that is, nothing but receptivity, and the form of that intuition may lie *a priori* in our faculty of representation, without being anything but the manner in which a subject is affected. But the connection (*conjunctio*) of anything manifold can never enter into us through the senses, and cannot be contained, therefore, already in the pure form of sensuous intuition, for it is a spontaneous act of the power of representation; and as, in order to distinguish this from sensibility, we must call it understanding, we see that all connecting, whether we are conscious of it or not, and whether we connect the manifold of intuition or several concepts together, and again, whether that intuition be sensuous or not sensuous, is an act of the understanding. This act we shall call by the general name of *synthesis*, in order to show that we cannot represent to ourselves anything as connected in the object, without having previously connected it ourselves, and that of all representations *connection* is the only one which cannot be given through the objets but must be carried out by the subject itself, because it is an act of its spontaneity.[2]

[1] T. M. Greene (ed), *Kant Selections*. (New York: Scribners' Sons, 1929), p. xxix.
[2] *Ibid.*, p. 73.

Knowledge arises, thus, from a number of synthesizing acts, e.g. time, space, substance, causation. This view of knowledge is a synthesis of rationalism and empiricism. The necessity the rationalist attributed to such concepts as substance is real, not illusory as the empiricists claimed. But the necessity is in the mind as the empiricists had maintained.

But though Kant provided Marx with the conception of an active mind, Kant's philosophy went too far toward idealism for Marx. Kant's analysis of knowledge as the synthetic activity of the mind led him to infer that man's world must necessarily be that of appearance. If what we suppose to be characteristics of external objects (e.g. substance) are merely synthetic activities of the mind, then the world as man knows it is phenomenal, not of reality-in-itself. Because his knowledge is an active formation of his world, man can never know the external reality as it is in itself. Knowledge as active implies, for Kant, knowledge only of appearance, never reality. It was at this point that Marx felt Kant had gone too far.

To Materialism Nature was allowed to be active, but the role of Thought was purely passive, limited to receiving what was "given" in the senses, and to excogitating upon that which was "given." It was Kantian and post-Kantian idealism which elucidated and emphasised the *constructive* role played by subjective *activity* – and carried this emphasis to the limit of extravagant exaggeration.[1]

Marx also found elements within Hegel which were useful in his own epistemology. We have seen how Marx conceived of both the object and subject as being active in knowledge. This conception came from Hegel whose ontology, he tells us, is that of "active (dialectical) Subject, not passive Substance." Substance for Hegel is living; it is the subject which has as its reality its own activity.

The living substance, further, is that being which is truly subject, or, what is the same thing, is truly realized and actual (*wirklich*) solely in the process of positing itself, or in mediating with its own self its transitions from one state or position to the opposite. . . . True reality is merely this process of reinstating self-identity, of reflecting into its own self in and from its other, and is not an original and primal unity as such, not an immediate unity as such. It is the process of its own becoming, the circle which presupposes its end as its purpose, and has its end for its beginning; it becomes concrete and actual only by being carried out, and by the end it involves.[2]

[1] T. Jackson, *Dialectics: The Logic of Marxism.* (London: M. Lawrence Company, 1936), pp. 44, 45.

[2] G. W. F. Hegel, *The Phenomenology of Mind.* (London: Allen and Unwin, 1955), pp. 80, 81. (Hereafter cited as *Phen.*).

With this view of substance, Hegel's epistemology necessarily involves the activity of the *object* in knowledge. For the object cannot be a merely passive substance upon which the act of knowledge is "perpetrated."

Hegel's epistemology begins as a criticism of other epistemologies, especially that of Kant. Hegel believed that one could not analyze thought from a neutral position as Kant had attempted. The analysis of thought, said Hegel, involves thought. For Hegel, Kant's analysis of knowledge implied real knowledge. To know the way the mind functions in cognition is knowledge. In his *Logic,* Hegel states:

> Kant undertook to examine how far the forms of thought were capable of leading to the knowledge of truth. In particular he demanded a criticism of the faculty of cognition as preliminary to its exercise. This is a fair demand if it means that even the forms of thought must be made an object of investigation. Unfortunately there soon creeps in the misconception of already knowing before you know, - the error of refusing to enter the water until you have learnt to swim. True, indeed, the forms of thought should be subjected to a scrutiny before they are used: yet what is this scrutiny but *ipso facto* a cognition? So that what we want is to combine in our process of inquiry the action of the forms of thought with a criticism of them. The forms of thought must be studied in their essential nature and complete development: they are at once the object of research and the action of that object. Hence they examine themselves: in their own action they must determine their limits, and point out their defects.[1]

Because of this divergence from Kant, Hegel starts at a different point in his epistemology. In order to know one does not first examine the instruments of knowledge (as Kant had done). Using this method we might never arrive at knowledge – which is what some critics have said of Kant's efforts. One begins, Hegel asserted, by beginning. To dig a hole, to put Hegel's view in metaphorical terms, one does not first examine the shovel, but puts the shovel into operation.

Hegel breaks with the traditional epistemological method of beginning with certainty and then working outward to knowledge of the external world. This was the special methodology of Descartes who began with certainty of the existence of the self and then proceeded to prove the existence of God and the external world from this basis. Hegel does not attempt to justify his starting point before starting. He continues to the end and then shows that his starting point was correct.

Knowledge for Hegel consists in the coming together of the object and the subject into a synthesis. Knowledge is a process whereby the

[1] G. W. F. Hegel, *The Logic of Hegel.* (Oxford: Oxford University Press, 1892), p. 84. (Hereafter cited as *Logic*).

object becomes another form of the subject. It is merely that in the process the object is *seen* as an opposition; at the conclusion of the process, object and subject are united. The subject externalizes itself in the object; the object returns to the subject. In Hegel's words:

The negative of the object, its cancelling its own existence, gets, for self-consious-ness, a positive significance; or, self-conciousness knows this nothingness of the object because on the one hand self-consciousness itself externalizes itself; for in doing so it establishes itself as object, or, by reason of the indivisible unity characterizing its self-existence, sets up the object as its self. On the other hand there is also this other moment in the process, that self-consciousness has just as really cancelled and superseded this self-relinquishment and objectification, and has resumed them into itself, and is thus at home with itself in its otherness as such. This is the movement of consciousness, and in this process consciousness is the totaliy of its moments.[1]

The most significant point in this whole discussion of Hegel's epistemology is that he conceives of knowledge, as did Kant, as an active process. The subject dirempts itself and returns to itself in knowing; knowledge is activity.

It is through action that spirit is spirit so as definitely to exist; it raises its existence into the sphere of thought and hence into absolute opposition, and returns out of it through and within this very opposition.[2]

4. MARX'S EPISTEMOLOGICAL METHOD

Epistemology, for Marx, is not merely an academic question. Man's knowledge of reality is a facet of his more comprehensive task of actively creating a world consonant with his complete realization. We find Marx's epistemology only within his discussion of other general topics. As was said earlier, Marx's epistemology is seldom set off by itself in a purely philosophic discussion. Marx's epistemology is to be found in the context of his entire system – in his theories of economics, his political theories, etc.

Marx's starting point in epistemology is not that of Cartesian doubt. This break from tradition is significant in that it did not suppose that the way to knowledge is from self-awareness, that the way to certainty is through doubt. Marx's idea seems to have been something like the following criticism of the method of doubt by a contemporary Marxist.

If we open almost any modern popular book on philosophy we find that the argument starts off by creating a certain atmosphere of *doubt*.

[1] G. W. F. Hegel, *Phen.*, pp. 789, 790.
[2] *Ibid.*, p. 797.

Thus Joad, in his *Guide to Philosophy*, begins with the question, "What do we know of the outside world?" He then proceeds to examine a number of statements embodying the "common-sense" view of the world, and concludes that "... it is reasonably certain that in the form in which we have just stated them, none of them is true." A similar path is followed by Bertrand Russell in many of his writings. We will take the form he gives the argument in his *Problems of Philosophy*.

In this book Russell starts off asking if there is "any knowledge in the world that is so certain that no reasonable man could doubt it?" To the philosopher in his study (who assumes, by the way, that he has an unquestioned title to "reasonableness") there seems very little of such knowledge indeed. This table, of whose "solid reality" the ordinary man is so strongly convinced – what do we know about it? True, we experience a certain feeling of "hardness" when we touch it, and we see various coloured images when, as we say, we look at the table from different angles and in different lights. But beyond these feelings and these images, and the fact of their association, the rest is mere inference. Whether or not there may be a good reason to believe in the existence of the "real table," or more generally in a material world, all that is primarily "given to us," all that we *know for certain*, are our sensations (Russell uses the word "sense-data"). Thus, Russell concludes, "whatever else may be doubtful, some at least of our immediate experiences seem absolutely certain." A "reasonable man" could doubt the existence of a material world as the cause of his sensations, but not the sensations themselves. ...

Idealist philosophers (including Russell, in his abovementioned book) are always stumbling over this difficulty, and then running away from it as hard as they can. It must be admitted that *starting* from a belief in nothing except "my" sensations it is very hard to "prove" the existence of anything else. But the true position is even worse than we have indicated. We may doubt the accuracy of our memories, even the continuity of thought required to complete a sentence, and thus arrive at a "philosophy" called "solipsism of the present moment." Needless to say its adherends are not to be found outside lunatic asylums! ...

If we are to avoid these self-destructive conclusions we must completely deny the line of argument which led to them. We must reject that innocent-looking philosophical doubt, which pretends to start with the minimum of assumptions, but really denies the existing world in order to replace it by arbitrary fantasies of the philosophy.[1]

Marx did not start with experience as the *indubitandum*, as the ideallists had done. He began with things, individuals and their material structures of existence. Thus in the *German Ideology*:

The premises from which we begin are not arbitrary ones, not dogmas, but real premises from which abstraction can only be made in the imagination. They are the real individuals, their activity and the material conditions under which they live, both those which they find already existing and those produced by their activity. These premises can thus be verified in a purely empirical way.[2]

[1] D. Guest, *Lectures on Marxist Philosophy*. (London: Lawrence and Wishart, 1963), pp. 21–23.
[2] K. Marx, *GI*, pp. 6, 7.

Things are the unquestionable basis of knowledge for Marx. But what are these "things?" They are entities existing independent of relation to other things. Marx proposes a realist basis for the existence of objects. Instead of objects depending for their existence upon mind, mental entities (ideas) are dependent upon objects for their existence.

Materialism is the recognition of "objects in themselves," or outside the mind; ideas and sensations are copies or images of these objects. The opposite doctrine (idealism) claims that objects do not exist "without the mind;" objects are "combinations of sensations." [1]

What is immediately presented to man's experience is a world of independently existing objects and their material relations. As Lenin was later to point out, Marxist epistemology differs both from idealism and agnosticism.

For the materialist the "factually given" is the outer world, the image of which is our sensations. For the idealist the "factually given" is sensation, and the outer world is declared to be a complex of sensations. For the agnostic the "immediately given" is also sensation, but the agnostic *does not go on* either to the materialist recognition of realty of the outer world, or to the idealist recognition of the world as our sensation.[2]

These independently existing objects are said by Marx to be of a material nature. In fact, this is the definition of "material" for Marx. The term is the opposite of ideal. "Material" means that which can exist apart from anything else, e.g. apart from relation to a mind; "ideal" means that which has reality only in relation to something else. It is material objects which bring about knowledge.

Matter is that which, acting upon our sense-organs, produces sensation; matter is the objective reality given to us in sensation. . . ." [3]

Marx did not attempt a complete *logical* proof of his epistemological point of departure. He simply seems to assume that the knowledge of things is so unquestionable, so much a part of accepted common sense, that no one could deny or doubt it.

To begin with *things* is ostensibly as justifiable as to begin with *experience*. Certainly the method of doubt has not served to bring certainty!

Marx does offer a justification of his epistemological methodology –

[1] V. Lenin, *Materialism and Empiro-Criticism.* (New York: International Publishers, 1927), p. 95.
[2] *Ibid.*, p. 175.
[3] *Ibid.*, p. 207.

possibly the only justification consistent with his principles. It is not a logical proof. He substantiates the validity of his theory of knowledge not at the beginning but at the conclusion of the theory. He proves his conception of knowledge to be correct by exhibiting its usefulness in man's chief task – the transformation of reality. A method of knowledge is sound if it assists man in his creation of a new world.

This is not *logical* but *practical* proof. This was also the form of Hegel's proof of his epistemology (proof at the end, not the beginning), as was seen previously. Such an "active" substantiation would seem to be even more significant within Marx's epistemology, for, as will become evident, knowledge *is* activity for Marx.

5. KNOWLEDGE AS ACTIVITY

Having seen Marx's starting point, we return to his conception of knowledge as activity. This conception came from both Kant and Hegel. They offered a view of mind as active which was absent in materialism. Materialism, Marx says in his first thesis on Feuerbach, correctly recognizes that all knowledge is based on sensations, thus emphasizing the activity of external objects affecting the senses. But activity is present, maintained Marx, at both poles of the knowledge process. Materialism had incorrectly viewed the mind as the passive instrument which merely receives, combines, and reflects upon sensations. Materialism had failed to see that man gains knowledge through *subjective activity*.

Reality, according to Marx, must be viewed as the result of the redirective activity of human beings in relation to changing conditions in external reality. Both the object and the subject are continually active; human history may be seen as a process in which changes in material reality create new needs which in turn bring about human transformations of material reality.

First, then, Marx takes up the Kantian idea of the activity of the mind in knowledge. In the first thesis on Feuerbach, when Marx speaks of the "active side" of the object developed by idealism, he has in mind the doctrine of the constitutive activity of the understanding as first developed by Kant. Kant's mistake, Marx felt, was to conclude from such activity of the mind in cognition that knowledge of reality is impossible. On the contrary, Marx maintained, the mind's activity in knowledge assures man's knowledge of the world, which is the joint creation of external reality and subjective activity.

Secondly, Marx had been further influenced by Hegel's philosophy in coming to his activist epistemology. Hegel had correctly discerned that object and subject are inter-active in knowledge. But Hegel had remained, said Marx, within idealism, where such a view involved no human, sensuous activity.

Kant had made the oppositional unity of Object and Subject the pivot of his whole system – but, inconsistently, he had conceived that their union was *active* and result-producing only on one side, the side of subjectivity. Hegel removed the inconsistency and built his system on the conception that it was not in the "pure" object or in the "pure" subject that the Truth lay, but in the *active inter-relation* between them, which relation produced a progressive transformation both of subject *and* of object. On the plane of Idealism this conception led straight to mysticism, and through mysticism to the negation of all rational Thought. Transferred, in an inverse form, to the plane of Materialism, this led straight to the Marxian world-conception.[1]

As with Hegel so Marx was to maintain that the possibility of knowledge arises from the common activity of subject and object. But whereas Hegel had made the subject primary, Marx held that both subject and object are equally important.

It is in relation to Hegel especially that we can see the uniqueness of Marx's conception of knowledge. For Hegel (and most philosophers) cognition involves or leads to no necessary *material* activity in the world. Knowledge is a process which leaves the world materially unchanged. For Marx, on the contrary, knowledge necessarily implies and makes possible "sensuous activity," practice.

C. E. M. Joad in his *Guide to Philosophy* has given us perhaps the best explanation of this activist element in Marxian epistemology.

There is no such thing, he [Marx] insists, as a knowing which is a mere contemplation of the outside world. The human being is like a coiled spring waiting to uncoil itself in action at the first touch of a stimulus from without. At the starting point of its action, it knows or is aware of the stimulus; but this knowledge, like the release of the spring, is only incidental. The true purpose of the human being's activity is not to know the stimulus but to change it. "Philosophers have only *interpreted* the world in various ways," Marx complains, "but the real task is to *alter* it." This is not to deny that we can know the outside world; in certain unrepresentative moments we may even be content with a mere knowing. But the knowing is not an end in itself; we know in order to act. Knowledge cannot be understood, nor does it occur independently of its relation to action, the object of which is to change what is known. A cat does not merely know a mouse; a farmer does not merely know a field of standing corn. Their real concern is not with knowledge, but with action, and the "knowing" is only an incident in a chain of events which ends in action. Action changes the environment acted upon; it also changes the agent; thus neither human nature nor the world is static; a continu-

[1] T. Jackson, *op. cit.*, p. 55.

ously changing agent knows a continually changing environment, and, by reason of his knowledge, gives it the impetus to further change. If knowing is the preliminary to action, matter is, for Marx its opportunity. He conceives of matter as a kind of raw material which is known in order that it may be transformed by the knowing individual into a completed product. There can, then, be no such thing as disinterested thought, thought which is merely concerned to know, and objective truth is a figment. "The question whether objective truth belongs to human thinking is not," Marx insists, "a question of theory, but a practical question. The truth, that is the reality and power of thought, must be demonstrated in practice. The contest as to the reality or non-reality of a thought which is isolated from practice, is a purely scholastic question." Since the purpose of knowledge is to change matter, that kind of knowledge is true which changes it sucessfully – that is to say, in accordance with the purposes which led us initially to concern ourselves with it. Finally, since knowing is continuous and changes what is known, the world is itself continually changing. As what is known changes, so does the knowledge that we have of the world. Hence both truth and reality develop, and, since it contains the principle of development within itself, Marx feels justified in appropriating Hegel's word "Dialectical" to describe his own philosophy of Materialism.[1]

Knowledge, for Marx, is that activity of man whereby he comes into interaction with the world and understands it so as to transform it. This is a total redefinition of knowledge. Knowledge is an active process of apprehension which is necessarily linked to transformation of reality. Subjective, non-active apprehension of external reality is knowledge; but it is incomplete – it is mere "interpretation," mere "criticism."

We must be clear at this point. Knowledge (for Marx)is *not* material transformation of reality. Knowledge, however, is necessarily related to such transformation. There is no complete cognition which is knowledge for knowledge sake.

Hence, knowledge is active in two senses. First, knowledge is an active inter-relationship between subject and object. Secondly, apprehension gained from this process must itself be active in nature. Ideas cannot be passive images; they must be active instruments.

6. MARX AND PRAGMATISM

Marx's epistemology has evident similarity to Pragmatism. It is in epistemology that Marxism and Pragmatism approximate one another most closely. The line of influence, here, is difficult to determine. Few of the leaders of Pragmatism ever referred to Marx as a source of their ideas. The relationship would seem to be indirect and subtle. It would

[1] C. E. M. Joad, *A Guide to Philosophy*. (New York: Dover, 1936), pp. 475, 476. Reprinted through permission of the publisher.

appear that Marxism and Pragmatism came to similar views independently.

In comparing the epistemology of Marxism and Pragmatism we shall take John Dewey as the representative of Pragmatism. Marx's conception of knowledge and truth have more in common, certainly, with Dewey than with James. James' emphasis on personal utility would distinguish his view from Marx. One interpreter of Marx, however, has differentiated Marxism from Pragmatism taking James' subjective view as representative.

> In Pragmatism, Marxism sees a complete annihilation of the criterion of truth which it proposes, namely, *objective* practice. It is true that Pragmatism likewise proposes practice as the criterion of truth, but when it speaks of "practice" it usually refers to *subjective* practice. For the Pragmatist that knowledge is true which "works for me," which appears "attractive to me," which fulfills the personal desires of the Pragmatist himself. For the Marxist, that knowledge is true which, when applied, is productive of progress and development in the objective world of material reality.[1]

Such comparison would seem less fruitful than a consideration of Marx and Dewey in relation to their theories of knowledge. Dewey's instrumentalism has objective features which are similar to Marx.

In the opening chapters of *The Quest for Certainty*, Dewey explains how the Greeks looked down on activity because of the unpleasantness connected with practical labor, the dishonor of the "working class," the association of activity with matter, and the exaltatation of the pure intellect and its activity as fundamentally concerned with the quest for certainty which is "absolute and unshakeable."

Activity, Dewey states, must forever be connected with the uncertain. Uncertainty is disliked not in itself but because it involves us in the perils of evil. Thus it was that in the Greek culture there came to be two realms of being. The inferior was that in which man could foresee and control the future outcome of events by means within his control. The superior realm was that in which uncontrollable events took place so as to testify to the presence and agency of superior powers.

Philosophy, Dewey asserts, inherited the second realm – the realm of religion. "Pure activity" came to be known as the rational impression of form on inferior matter, while action belonged to the realm of decay and passing. The perfect was the complete, unchanging; that which changes is material.

From these views came the opinion that knowledge deals with the

[1] C. J. McFadden, *op. cit.*, p. 77.

antecedently real. Knowledge is the correspondence between thought and the real. Knowledge is the standard of the reality of all other types of experience. What is known is antecedent to the act of cognition and is totally unaffected by such. Philosophy, Dewey maintains, has accepted three aspects of these views:

> The first, that certainty, security, can be found only in the fixed and unchanging; the second, that knowledge is the only road to that which is intrinsically stable and certain; the third, that practical activity is an inferior sort of thing, necessary simply because man's animal nature and the necessity of winning subsistence from the environment.[1]

The trouble with the Greek thinkers was that they tended, due to the view expressed above, to accept thing as they appeared. They were not deficient in theory but in perceptual transformation. They thought that by taking the ordinary material of perception and systematizing it they could reach the immutable essence of things.

The real advance of science, says Dewey, came with the recognition that the subject-matter of experience must be changed. By means of apparatus, science gets away from simple perception. Science uses thought, not as the Greeks did to discover properties of entities, but to *change* data into objects. The key to progress in knowledge, then, is the *transformation* of the "material to serve" into meaningful objects.

One might get the impression that Dewey is establishing science as *the* structure and method of thought. At times he approaches that. But, elsewhere, he is careful to make distinctions between scientific and other modes of thinking. Science, he states, resolves objects and nature as a whole into facts stated exclusively in terms of quantities which may be handled in calculation. It is limited only to certain purposes. The scientific procedure is not best in all cases. The closer we approach the individual and unique aspects of experience, the less adequate is this metric method of procedure.

We shall attempt to outline the cognitive experience [according to Dewey] into its generic features. First, there is the confrontation of the data, the sense qualities. These are elements *to be* known; they are challenges to knowing and set problems for investigation. These are the residue from past experience; we do not start empty-handed. "What one person and one group accomplish becomes the standing ground and starting point of those who succeed them." [2]

[1] J. Dewey, *The Quest for Certainty.* (New York: Putnam, 1929), p. 51.
[2] J. Dewey, *A Common Faith.* (New Haven: Yale University Press, 1934), p. 50.

The dificulty here, of course, is the fact that mind only arises on the occasion of the doubtful. It would appear that there can be no residuum if the mind is called forth only on certain occasions; mind creates a calm and fades away into inactivity. It seems clear that Dewey wants to "load" the event itself so that it is both retentive of the past and attentive to the future. He speaks of the event as being "both expectant and commemorative."

When we confront the data, ideas arise in us. The data locate the problem and a thought is evoked which outlines an operation for the settlement of the difficulty. What data are selected is determined by the nature of the problem. The mass of data must be resolved into some meaningful order because in their original mode they are obscure, perplexing, and fragmentary. By themselves they fail to answer a need which has arisen.

Ideas are anticipatory plans of action which take effect in concrete *reconstructions* of data. They arise from the particular situation. They are not properties of things or original elements of the mind. They are attitudes of response taken toward non-ideal things. Their validity is measured by their capacity to effect the transformation which they propose. There is no *a priori* test as to their validity. They originate in human action and must be tested and improved in the course of that action.

Following upon the idea as anticipatory plan there comes the transformation of the material into an object of knowledge. This is a constructed, existentially produced object. The knowledge process is partially determinate of the final result; *cognition is not passive reception but active reshaping and change according to an idea.* Reflection or thought is, in this way, an intermediate element between a temporally prior experience wherein certain factors have become discordant and a later situation "which has been constituted out of the first situation by means of acting on the findings of reflective inquiry." The direct outcome of reflection is the reorganization of a situation which confers upon the event new tinctures of meaning. These results can be used in subsequent investigations.

The object of knowledge, that which results, is only eventual. It is an outcome of directed, experimental operations. It does not exist before the act of knowing. As we have seen, there are materials which do exist before the activity. But the object to which the knowledge process moves only appears at the end.

Dewey is critical of epistemological theories which see knowledge as an activity whereby we are reminded of something we already know. He disagrees with such theories as Locke's which tested all reflective ideas by reduction to original "simple ideas." Because the search for knowledge is always forward-moving it can never attain certainty. The "quest for certainty" is doomed to failure. All that is ever attained are temporary, tentative results. These results are never allowed to solidify into norms for future knowledge. They are merely instruments for new inquiry.

Having seen Dewey's theory of knowledge we can now attempt a comparison with Marx. In both men the discussion of epistemology is to be found in the context of their general writings. Very seldom does either man write exclusively on epistemological issues. The theory of knowledge, for both, is part of a larger problem.

For both Marx and Dewey reality is composed of *things and their relations in process*. For Marx the focal point is the economic relations, while for Dewey the focus is on the neutral "event." Marx emphasizes economic relations because he sees these as the primary determinants of human existence. The "event" would appear to be the key term for Dewey because it contains all the ingredients necessary to his system. The event encompasses a problem, thought, an idea, transformation of the given according to the idea, and resultant solution.

Though each of these men centers on different aspects, their definition of reality is essentially the same. It is this context of reality within which knowledge plays its role. Given that reality is made up of things and their relations in process, then knowledge has as its function the guidance and control of this process. For both Dewey and Marx knowledge directs the activity of *transforming* reality. This activity of knowledge is tested for truth by witnessing whether or not the proposed changes actually bring about the end desired. That element of knowledge is true which helps to attain the desired transformation.

Disparity between the views of Marx and Dewey occurs in terms of the ends served by knowledge – the kind of transformation desired. For Marx, reality must be changed in terms of the ownership of the means of production by all and the establishment of a communistic form of society. Dewey's proposed end is a democratic society where progress is brought about through "creative intelligence." Notwithstanding these diverse goals, the means is knowledge.

CHAPTER III

ACTIVITY AND PHILOSOPHY

> Philosophers have only interpreted the world differently; the point is to change it.
>
> (*Theses on Feuerbach*)

I. INTRODUCTION

In this chapter we shall investigate the relation of theory and practice in Marx's philosophy. In the context of Marx's system, theory and practice refer to the theory and practice of transforming society. Society means, for Marx, the economic and political relations in the existing state.

We must deal with Hegel's political philosophy in this section because Marx created his political theory in contrast and opposition to Hegel. It would be incorrect either to picture Marx as nothing but a warmed-over version of Hegel, or to see no relation between Hegel and Marx. Certainly, the philosophy of Hegel was a dominant influence on Marx, though not the only one. Professor Hook is probably correct in stating that the nature of this influence was methodological and doctrinal as well as psychological. Therefore, to understand Marx's theory of the transformation of the state we must see the background out of which it came.

2. HEGEL'S THEORY OF THE STATE

For man, in Hegel's thought, there are three spheres of existence: abstract right, subjective right (morality), and concrete right (ethical life). Abstract right is the sphere of objective reality in which the "person" manifests his particular will and is therefore an object for others. In the subjective sphere the person becomes a "subject" and the personality exists not for others but for himself. Concrete right is the culmination and perfection of the subject existing in and for himself. The objective manifestation of this concrete right is the State.

The State is the actuality of the ethical Idea. It is ethical mind qua the substantial will manifest and revealed to itself, knowing and thinking itself, accomplishing what it knows and in so far as it knows it. The state exists immediately in custom, self-consciousness, knowledge, and activity, while self-consciousness in virtue of its sentiment towards the state finds in the state, as its essence and the end and product of its activity, its substantive freedom.[1]

From the French Revolution Hegel drew the lesson that the individual cannot bring political emancipation, only the State can do this. Because of the many competing interests contained within the State a system of free government cannot be attained by single interests but can come only by the imposition of a supreme power over all struggling interests. Hegel believed democracy to be the tyranny of the many over the one. Hegel's *Philosophy of Right* is written to counter the claims of the various powers existent in his day. Each of these separate powers he saw as destructive of freedom and right. His treatise on right is intended as proof that man has reached the place where reason can be realized in the State. Therefore, philosophy, as the explication of this notion of the State is meant to reconcile men to the actual. Of the *Philosophy of Right*, Hegel said:

This book, then, containing as it does the science of the state, is to be nothing other than the endeavour to apprehend and portray the state as something inherently rational. As a work of philosophy, it must be poles apart from an attempt to construct a state as it ought to be. The instruction which it may contain cannot consist in teaching the state what it ought to be; it can only show how the state, the ethical universe, is to be understood. [2]

The World Soul entrusts a particular nation with a moment of the Idea and calls for the complete manifestation of the Idea as the self-developing of the World Mind continues. This activity of the World Soul makes each State sovereign, with no authority beyond it. States are related as sovereign powers who make agreements but do not, in this way build up a body of objective laws. States construct only contracts in their inter-relations and they stand above these contracts.

A. Sovereignty

At the head of the State stands a Sovereign – a Monarch. Sovereignty assures that each sphere of interest is not left separated and self-subsistent but is related to all others so that each is co-determined by the rest. A Monarch, says Hegel, is not deduced but is self-originating. Morris interprets Hegel's view in a succinct passage:

The selection of the Prince, too, is withdrawn from the struggles of factions and the mutations of caprice and referred to Nature, by the rule of hereditary suc-

[1] G. W. F. Hegel, *The Philosophy of Right*. (Oxford: Clarendon Press, 1942), p. 155. (Hereafter cited as *PR*). By permission of the Clarendon Press, Oxford.
[2] *Ibid.*, p. 11.

cession according to the law of primogeniture. The Monarch thus gives no more reason for his right to be, than does the State itself. In this, as also in the power of independent self-determination, is found at once the majesty of the Monarch and the majesty of the State.[1]

The State must be exemplified, according to Hegel, in an individual. This person is raised above all that is particular and conditional. Such an exalted individual is the only adequate manifestation of the Idea of the state. As the highest expression of the Idea, the Monarch *is* the State. As the highest person, however, he is not valued in his particularity. Monarch for Hegel is more an office than any individual occupying that office.

In a completely organized state, it is only a question of the culminating point of formal decision (and a natural bulwark against passion. It is wrong therefore to demand objective qualities in a monarch); he has only to say "yes" and dot the "i", because the throne should be such that the significant thing in its holder is not his particular make-up.[2]

If the State is to be unified, all individual wills must be expressed in the Supreme Will embodied in one person. The relation of the Monarch to the people is that of an organism to its parts. In an organism there can be no conflict between the interest of the part and the interest of the whole. The proper function of the part is to be an organ of the whole. In just such a way the institutions of society, in Hegel's view, are to be subservient to the absolute authority of the Monarch.

B. Civil Society

The distinction between State and Civil Society is not to be found in Plato and is perhaps the influence of Locke on Hegel's thought. Such a demarcation of spheres is at least implicit in Locke. For Hegel, civil society is the arena of combat between individual interests. Here the individual will seeks unrestrained satisfaction. The elements of civil society are related to one another by means of a mechanical subordination of particular interests to a universal law for the protection of all. In society man is governed, while in the State man is self-governed. The change from civil society to State is well described by Morris.

This change is brought about when the relatively mechanical relation of enforced obedience or external legality, by which in the sphere of Civil Society the individual is outwardly and visibly kept in his place, there is added the inward grace of an enlightened and truly self-knowing will; when the public interest is com-

[1] G. S. Morris, *Hegel's Philosophy of the State and of History*. (Chicago: Scott, Foresman and Company, 1902), p. 95.
[2] G. W. F. Hegel, *PR.* pp. 288, 289.

prehended, outward obedience becomes the natural and spontaneous garb and expression of an inward spirit, of an all pervading ethos, and mere government is changed to moral and substantial self-government.[1]

Civil Society is the State on its external side. Society is not left behind at the level of the State. The State is a universal which breaks forth into difference. This area of self-seeking and conflict is necessary for the State; this *is* the State in externality or objectivity. Civil society serves as a school to reveal to man that his good is integrally related to the good of all. It is more than a school, however, in that it allows for the continued expression of uneducated desire. It can never be merely identified with the State; its continuance is a necessary moment in the State's life.

Society becomes State when the law which is realized unconsciously in the former becomes the object of conscious will in the latter. This bringing to consciousness must be done by those already aware of the law as an explicit object. This necessitates the existence of classes: the educators and the uneducated. Thus, society is not only a stage of development for Hegel, but also a class. There can be no State (or any reality) without the imposition of form (law) on matter (persons). For both Plato and Hegel the metaphysical divisions of their systems become classes within the State. Society, therefore, is related to the State in two ways: 1) the State is an external and superior authority which subordinates the interests of society, and 2) the State is the immanent end of society.

C. The Individual and Freedom

Hegel reinterprets freedom as the service of the will to the State. It is not the power to do what one likes according to individual desire; it is making the general will one's personal will in such a way that what is enforced is now desired.

The individual comes ... to recognize in the universal the groundwork and substance of his own spirit, and to subordinate his activities to it as to their (proximately) final end. In other words, in the State, as the actualization of concrete freedom, neither is the universal established in authority and carried into realization in abstraction from the particular interests, opinions, and volitions of individuals, nor do the latter live, as private persons, in exclusive devotion to their special interests; the rather, the universal enters concretely into their wills, and consciously determines the direction of their activity. "The tremendous strength and depth of the principle of subjectivity, or private personality, is allowed to be carried to its fullest and extreme development, and is yet at the same time re-

[1] G. S. Morris, *op. cit.*, p. 84.

duced into substantial harmony and unity with, and made a vehicle of realization for, the universal Will of man.[1]

The State is the manifestation of concrete freedom in which the particular interests of the individual are united with the universal aim of man. Only the individual's caprice, Hegel contends, is restrained according to the more universal will. The individual's real will is emancipated.

As the self forms a rational structure of morality which is incorporated into law and custom, it is sustained by the State. The State as the concretion and foundation of morality is its own end and the individual's highest duty is to be a member of the State. The State is the common Self or the general will. Since the State is objective mind the individual gains reality only as a member of this entity. Individuals are not complete in themselves but must will the universal and aim at unity with the universal. Individual interests, says Hegel, are not to be destroyed or suppressed, they are to be put in correspondence with the universal so that both are maintained.

Since for Hegel the state is as it should be, political philosophy no longer advocates change, but teaches acceptance. Philosophy counsels that the state be recognized as a moral universe. The task of philosophy becomes that of "reconciling men to the actual." The philosopher discovers the meaning of the universe and becomes almost a divine officer. Philosophy does not "do" anything more than bring understanding, reconciliation to the present conditions. Philosophy neither sows nor reaps in the thought of Hegel.

On Hegel's view the outstanding fact about the laws that govern the universe is that they are the expression of the Absolute Idea, of spirit, of thought. It is the Idea, it is thought, which is, in Hegel's phrase, the demiurge of reality. To change reality you must change thought of society, and eventually to preserve and safeguard society in its present form, you must preserve and safeguard its thought.[2]

Thus, for Hegel, if philosophy brings about any change (though this is not its explicit function), then it does so only by changing thought. We shall see that this is the point where Marx diagrees most radically with Hegel. For Marx philosophical theory must necessarily be related to activity, to practice.

[1] *Ibid.*, pp. 82, 83.
[2] A. C. Macintyre, *Marxism, An Interpretation.* (London: SCM Press, 1953), pp. 30, 31.

3. MARX'S DIAGNOSIS OF THE STATE

The state in Marx's conception is the synthesis of opposition between two antagonistic classes in society. It is the instrument of a propertied class against a propertyless class.

> The state according to Hegel is both "rational and necessary." For the Marxians, it is not only *not* in any sense "rational" and binding because self-imposed upon all those within its boundaries, as Hegel thinks, but on the contrary, it is for the non-ruling class, which constitutes the great majority, a thing very much opposed to their interests, and *the chief instrument by which they are kept in bondage.* It is manifestly "necessary" in the sense (also used by Hegel), that its appearance was inevitable in the course of social development. In this sense, its diasppearance is also necessary.[1]

Hegel's acceptance of the existing state leads Marx to look upon him as the most profound expression of bourgeois, capitalist thought. Marx sees the state as proof of the irreconcilability of opposing classes. The state represents the interests of the ruling class interpreted as if they were the interests of all.

In strict departure from Hegel, Marx says the nature of the state is determined by empirical discovery not idealistic logic. Marx himself came to his own conception of the state through personal observation. In his early life he had concurred with Hegel's judgment that the state is essentially the merging of all interests. However, when he became editor of the *Rheinische Zeitung* he began reporting the daily activities of the government and soon discovered that Hegel's optimism about the state (being the expression of all classes) was illusory. Marx broke from his earlier position after the debates over wood-theft.

Persons owning large tracts of land had brought their case into the Rhenish Provincial Assembly; they asked that wood-theft be made a penal offense. They were not able to watch over their land reserves so they asked that the law be more strict with wood-thieves. It was in this dispute where Marx first forged the beginning of his theory of the state. How, he asked, could the state ignore its duty to the wood-stealers themselves who were critizens? He believed that now he saw the real nature of the state – an agency for the protection of the wealthy!

Historically, Marx believed, there had been a primitive communistic society existing between men. As agriculture had developed it had become necessary for the separation of land-holdings. Thus had arisen

[1] R. Cooper, *The Logical Influence of Hegel on Marx.* (Seattle: Washington University Press, 1925), p. 138.

private property. From such roots had sprung capitalism and modern bourgeois society. In capitalism man is defined by self-interest.

Marx disagrees with most of Hegel's political system. In Marx's thought there is no distinction between state and civil society.

Marx implies that the people should be sovereign as opposed to Hegel's Monarch. According to Marx, a new society can only be created by the people not by a single ruler.

4. THE CURE OF SOCIETY

A. General Method

The cure of society for Marx is in direct relation to its nature. If man is to transform society he must first comprehend it correctly. Thus there is a necessity for theory. Theory and the understanding it brings is an integral part of the method of society's cure.

But theory, says Marx, must in every instance lead to action. We have seen this element present in Marx's epistemology. Knowledge is directly and essentially related to the transformation of reality. Theory, as an aspect of knowledge, enables man to change society. Every facet of Marx's system is both historical and critical, i.e. it both describes the material conditions of human existence and shows how the material basis of present life must be transformed. The truth of materialism, as a thesis, is to be realized in its own negation. The capitalistic mode of production which Marx describes is to be revolutionized into communistic modes.

Contrary to the belief of some, Marx considered theory a very important element. He and Engels understood very well the significance of an adequage theoretical basis for their program of change. It was their practice to study past activities to guide their present theory.

In a small essay to which they both contributed (Germany: Revolution and Counter-Revolution) they worked out in theory the reasons why the earlier revolution had failed to make substantial changes in political and economic structure. They describe the prevailing conditions in 1847 as a theoretical preliminary to action.

This, then, was Marx's general method of curing society: first one studied the past (both the distant and the immediate past) and thereby came to a theory concerning the conditions prevaillng and the attempted methods of solution; secondly, this theory was then put into effect by transforming society according to its principles.

B. Philosophy

Philosophy, for Marx, is an instrument of change. Marx is influenced here by Feuerbach who also conceived of philosophy as social activity. Marx recognized the importance of theory. His main interest was that philosophy be more than mere theory – that it become a force of transformation.

Philosophy in Marx's system is not destroyed but completely transformed. Marcuse contends that Marx is one of the various forms of the negation of philosophy which followed Hegel's system. In a sense this is true. Marx was desirous of destroying philosophy as *mere* theoretical activity. It is in this same sense that Kant desired to destroy metaphysics, by showing it an impossible task as earlier attempted. But as Kant redefined and transformed the meaning and enterprise of metaphysics, Marx defined and reinterpreted philosophy.

Marx explicitly condemns a merely theoretical philosophy. He criticized German thinkers because they had done no more than theorize. "German criticism," he said, "has, right up to its latest efforts, never quitted the realm of philosophy." [1] Here he is using the word philosophy to mean mere theory. For such men, said Marx, philosophy has only the role of describing the world. "When reality is depicted, philosophy as an independent branch of activity loses its medium of existence." [2]

Concerning the role of philosophy, Marx and Edgar Bauer were in especially vehement opposition. Bauer had stated that philosophy is too practical. To this Marx made a scathing reply.

> It rather seems, however, that philosophy, precisely because it was only the transcendent, abstract expression of the actual situation, by reason of its transcendency and abstraction, by reason of its *imaginary difference* from the world, must have imagined it had left the actual situation and real human beings too far below. On the other hand, it seems that because philosophy is not really different from the world it could not give any *real opinion* on it, it could not bring any real differentiating force to act upon it and could therefore not interfere practically, but had to be satisfied at the best with a practice *in abstracto*. Philosophy was over-practical only in the sense that it soared above practice.[3]

Whenever Marx speaks of philosophy so as to disparage it, he is attacking that kind of philosophy which merely theorizes, which merely describes existing conditions without leading to their transformation.

Philosophy for Marx is *social* philosophy. Philosophy must necessa-

[1] K. Marx, *GI*, p. 4.
[2] *Ibid.*, p. 15.
[3] K. Marx, *HF*, pp. 56, 57.

rily be a study of man's social relations since these are his very essence. Man is a social animal; his being is constituted by his relation to other beings. But this is not to say that philosophy in Marx becomes economics or sociology. There is an inextricable relationschip between philosophy and the social scene, but philosophy does not *become* sociology or economics.

Also, philosophy does not become for Marx the active transformation of society. Philosophy must necessarily be linked to such transformation to be acceptable and valid, but the two are not identical. Philosophy leads to action; philosophy is not action *per se*.

> When Marxism speaks of the "unity of thought and action," it does not intend to imply that thought and action are one and the same thing. It does mean, however, that thought and action are inseparably united.[1]

According to Marx, for there to be a truly significant transformation of society, there must be philosophers and theorists who lead this transformation. Marx stated that one of the functions of socialists and communists was to act as theorists for the revolutionary class.

> As the Economists are the scientific representatives of the bourgeois class, so the Socialists and Communists are the Theorists of the proletarian class.[2]

The philosophical theorist is to point up the dialectical, revolutionary elements in the present order. Marx saw communists as the most advanced theorists.

For Marx theoretical activity is a necessary complement to practical activity. Practice must be guided by some insight into reality. And, on the other side of the coin, practice leads the discovery of more and more connections and relations in nature, that is, it leads to theory.

Even as early as the doctoral dissertation Marx had been discontent with philosophy separated from activity. As Marx hammered out his conception of reality it became clear to him that theory and practice must be united. This point would seem to be most consistent with the principles of his dialectical materialism. If, as Marx asserts, the *logos* or reason of the world moves concretely in reality, then it is a dialectically moving idea within nature and cannot be discovered in contemplative detachment. The structure of reality (since it is a dynamic, transforming element) can only be discerned by implanting oneself in reality

[1] C. J. McFadden, *op. cit.*, p. 69.
[2] K. Marx, *The Poverty of Philosophy*. (Chicago: C. H. Kerr, 1913), p. 136.

through sensuous practice. The basis for such ideas Marx discovered even in his early study for the dissertation.

> Marx's thesis for his doctorate, which deals in detail with Epicurus' transformation of the atomic theory of Democritus, is in fact part of his study of what happened to Greek philosophy after Aristotle. What happened to Greek philosophy is that it became practical. It turned from speculative metaphysics to ethics. This suggests the solution of Marx's problem. Hegel has in principle completed the task of speculative philosophy. But Hegel's philosophy remains in the realm of speculation, of the ideal. What has to be done is to realise the ideal in the world, not simply of thought, but of material reality. Hegel's theory must be converted into Marx's practice. This is Marx's problem.[1]

Philosophy must become a partner with practice in the changing of the world.

C. Marxism and Pragmatism

We earlier found noteworthy similarity between Marx's and Dewey's theories of knowledge. Their conceptions of philosophy's role also bear striking resemblance.

The most comprehensive context of Dewey's conception of philosophy is that of "experience." This is the term he uses to define and identify reality. It is within experience (as for Hegel) that everything occurs. Dewey defines experience explicitly; it is, he says, "the function of developing and perfecting value, instead of the function of knowing an unalterable object ..." [2]

From this and other passages we can be quite sure that the act of knowing is not primary for Dewey. Human experience is richer than the cognitive aspect; it includes habit, aesthetic enjoyment, and other elements.

That state where man is in uncontemplative awareness is, for Dewey, aesthetic. Every experience is aesthetic insofar as it is final or arouses no search for questions or some other type of experience. Man's common experience brings satisfactions. But he must not identify the mere fact of being liked with the value of the object liked. Values are not eternally in Being apart from standards and judgments made by man. Value cannot be correlated with liking but only with those which reflection approves. Valuation assumes the form of looking to those things which we enjoy, judging which are the best, and controlling their presence. We are often in the presence of the satisfying; reflection informs us of what is truly satisfactory.

[1] A. C. Macintyre, *op. cit.*, p. 39.
[2] J. Dewey, *The Influence of Darwin on Philosophy.* (New York: Holt, 1910), p. 222.

Criticism is necessary for the presence of true value. Criticism occurs whenever, instead of being rapt by the value-object, we raise questions as to its presence, its worth, or its probable duration.

The goal of knowledge is to resolve difficulty and return to that former aesthetic calm; "thinking is the actual transition from the problematic to the secure, as far as that is intentionally guided." [1]

We cannot over-emphasize either the valuational-aesthetic or the cognitive-reflective in Dewey's system. To make one appear as supreme, is to misconstrue Dewey's intention. As mere having is less than knowing, so the fulfillment of experience is more than knowing.

Criticism is integrally related to the possession of the valuable. By its operation, satisfying states are transformed into satisfactory experiences. This function of criticism is the designated task of philosophy.

> Philosophy is inherently criticism, having its distinctive position among various modes of criticism in its generality; a criticism of criticisms, as it were. Criticism is discriminating judgment, careful appraisal, and judgment is appropriately termed criticism wherever the subject-matter of discrimination concerns goods or values.[2]

Criticism (philosophy) is an activity common to all experience. It is not a formal discipline of the classroom, or as Dewey says, "it is not a matter of formal treatises, published articles, or taking up important matters for consideration in a serious way." Criticism takes place whenever value is pondered, questioned, or estimated.

Philosophy's task is to judge as to satisfactions which come to man, in an attempt to regulate the future appreciation of those experiences considered good. By estimating the value of certain states, philosophy allows more freedom and security in selecting, appropriating and excluding objects of belief, conduct and contemplation. The aim of criticism is a more intense and more complete appreciation of the meanings present in experience.

Criticism, as referred to above, is not the meaning we commonly give to the word. Its meaning is something more like reflective judgment upon the elements of our common life. But philosophy also is a specifically critical function, according to Dewey. It criticizes "beliefs, institutions, customs, policies" with respect to their bearing upon value. By taking regard of the causes and consequences of values it assists in their emancipation and expansion.

[1] J. Dewey, *The Quest for Certainty*, (New York: Minton, Balch and Company, 1929), p. 227.

[2] J. Dewey, *Experience and Nature*. (New York: Dover, 1958), p. 398.

One of Dewey's most provocative papers dealing with the role of philosophy is entitled, "The Need for a Recovery of Philosophy." It is here that Dewey calls for a new type of philosophic enterprise. It is my feeling that this conception of philosophy is one of the most significant of Dewey's contributions. Also, it is here that he is most in agreement with Marx's view of philosophy. A part of Dewey's theory of philosophy is that it should present relevant ideals to society.

If we are to have a philosophy which will intervene between attachment to rule of thumb muddling and devotion to a systematized surbordiantion of intelligence to pre-existent ends, it can be found only in a philosophy which finds the ultimate measure of intelligence in consideration of a desirable future and in search for the means of bringing it progressively into existence.[1]

Philosophy, says Dewey, must take its cue from empirical science which has taught us that it is possible to gain power to direct the consequences which flow naturally in the course of events. Philosophy, similarly, must become not merely a contemplative survey of the past but an outlook to future possibilities with the intention of attaining the better and avoiding the worse.

Philosophers, says Dewey, have the peculiar conviction that there is some other road than that of action directed by intelligence, to achieve human ideals and purposes. It is for this reason that philosophy has contributed so little to bringing about an integration between our knowledge of the world and the intelligent direction of what we do.

The evolution of philosophy into a discipline or field of study has added to its general ineffectiveness. It has become something to be thought. Many of its problems have become pseudo-concerns, unconnected with common life. Direct preoccupation with contemporary difficulties, states Dewey, is left to literature and politics. Philosophy becomes enraptured with the study of the past. And, as is always true, to dwell upon the past for its own sake is "to substitute the reminiscence of old-age for effective intelligence."

In light of philosophy's general impotency at present, what is to be the nature of the necessary change? Is philosophy to remain merely the giving of ideals, the inspiring by means of vision? At times Dewey speaks in these terms. But the most significant conception of philosophy in Dewey's thought is that of an *active* intellectual enterprise related to practice.

Dewey's view at this point appears to have two aspects. First, he

[1] J. Dewey, *Creative Intelligence.* (New York: Holt, 1917), p. 29.

wishes to maintain that philosophy's greatest contribution to the transformation of society is in the area of theory. Secondly, philosophy has signifiance as a method of approach to social problems. "Philosophy," he asserts, "recovers itself when it ceases to be a device for dealing with the problems of philosophers and becomes a method, cultivated by philosophers, for dealing with the problems of men." [1]

Philosophy must not remain a merely abstract enterprise. It must, to be consistent with Dewey's system, become related to action. Even when he is most insistent on philosophy's remaining exclusively a vision, he also includes the necessity that philosophy be joined with creative transformation of reality. Vision and imagination apart from action "resolve nothing."

Dewey is very sensitive to the close relation between means and ends. Ideas could be destroyed if given the wrong application. Even the conception of where and how to test ideas must come from philosophy. The philosophic enterprise is necessarily related to action.

> Ideas are worthless except as they pass into actions which rearrange and reconstruct in some way, be it little or large, the world in which we live. To magnify thought and ideas for their own sake apart from what they do (exept, once more esthetically) is to refuse to learn the lesson of the most authentic kind of knowledge – the experimental – and it is to reject the idealism which involves responsibility. To praise thinking above action because there is so much ill-considered action in the world is to help maintain the kind of a world in which action occurs for narrow and transient purposes.[2]

Philosophy, for Dewey, is theory that strives toward active control of man's environment. This does not mean that theory becomes practice or control. Both theory and practice are separate and equally necessary elements. Wisdom depends upon acquaintance with the two spheres of intelligent thought and practical means. Philosophy, as thought, must be concerned with the enlightened transformation of life for the better.

Our earlier investigation of Marx revealed that his conception of philosophy as leading to action was embodied in his own life activity. His struggle in revolutionary action was the logical outcome of his theoretical study of society. Likewise, Dewey also lived the idea that philosophy must be more than intellectual, must relate itself to society's improvement. His work in the educational sphere remains a strong influence. His active participation not only in education, but in political

[1] *Ibid.*, p. 65.
[2] J. Dewey, *The Quest for Certainty*. p. 48.

affairs, administrative situations, and so forth, testify to his conviction of the necessity of an essential relation between philosophy and practice.

The point at which the views of Marx and Dewey coincide is in seeing philosophy's role in social change as the giving of understanding, the clarification of goals, and the designation of means. With both men philosophy is the intellectual preliminary to practical activity.

As we saw earlier, Marx and Dewey differ as to the goals toward which activity is directed. They agree that philosophy should play an active role in the revolutionizing of the world. For Dewey the goal is a democratic society; for Marx a communistic society.

D. The Revolutionary Transformation of Society

We now turn our attention to Marx's theory of transforming the present state. Marx's system contains no metaphysical concept of the state. For him the state is an evil to be destroyed not a concept to be systematized. His primary thrust, then, is in terms of the method of revolutionizing the present structure and bringing it into conformity with man's deepest needs. The technique of change for Marx is the dialectic.

Dialectical laws, said Marx, are abstracted from facts. They have no absolute, superior reality; they serve merely as guides to further study and action. The dialectic is not primarily a doctrine but a movement – an activity! Marx believed that if dialectical materialism stated the laws of historical evolution correctly it could be generalized from the past to the present. In this way dialectic could predict the ultimate appearance of a socialist society. Dialectic, however, not only predicts but also calls for men to *produce* its predictions.

Dialectic, according to Marx, does not produce revolution, men do. Revolution is brought about through the use of the class-struggle which has historically been a corrupting force but is now used as an instrument for its own destruction. By class (proletarian) action the moment of opposition is changed into a phase of development. Contrary to the view of others, Marx maintained that change was to be accomplished not by a political party but by a class.

To bring about the conditions conducive to truly human existence, said Marx, it is necessary to destroy the class structure and establish communal ownership of all goods. The agency which is to destroy the bourgeois rule is the proletariat – the working class. The proletariat can speak for all men because it destroys all classes; the proletariat is the negation of all classes and therefore represents the universal interest. Because the proletariat receives no benefits from the class-system it rises above it. Both the proletariat and the bourgeoisie (propertied class) are in a state of alienation from man's true nature, but only among the proletariat is this estrangement consciously recognized and critically attacked.

The proletariat is that group of persons wholly devoid of humanity, who stand above the class structure in criticism and desire its destruction. The proletariat can represent the whole of society according to Marx.

For each new class which puts itself in the place of one ruling before it, is compelled, merely in order to carry through its aim, to represent its interest as the common interest of all the members of society, put in an ideal form; it will give its ideas the form of universality, and represent them as the only rational, universally valid ones. The class making a revolution appears from the very start, merely because it is opposed to a *class*, not as a class but as the representative of the whole of society; it appears as the whole of society; it appears as the whole mass of society confronting the one ruling class. It can do this because, to start with, its interest really is more connected with the common interest of all other non-ruling classes, because under the pressure of conditions its interest has not yet been able to develop as the particular interest of a particular class. Its victory, therefore, benefits also many individuals of the other classes which are not winning a dominant position, but only in so far as it now puts these individuals in a position to raise themselves into the ruling class.[1]

Marx believed that his appraisal of the proletariat had been borne out in history. He thought that in the transformation of society it had always been the working class who showed themselves able to be true revolutionaries. His study of the German revolution convinced him that the proletariat had distinguished itself "in showing upon every occasion that revolutionary boldness and readiness for action, in which any party headed by, and composed principally of petty tradesmen, will always be deficient." [2]

The first step toward a truly human society, proclaimed Marx, involves the freeing of the state from all ideas of the ruling class, that is, political emancipation. But *complete* transformation of capitalist society involves the final destruction of the state – the emancipation of communism.

The new form of society – communism – is created by the proletariat's destruction of private property which thereby establishes communal ownership and blends the interest of each into the whole. Now

[1] K. Marx, *GI*, p. 41.
[2] K. Marx, *Selected Works.* (New York: International Publishers, no date), p. 80.

for the first time man can realize his true nature as a social creature. The common good is recognized as the individual's good. Socialized life does not destroy individual value, it merely enhances it and uses it for the whole, according to Marx. Man thus becomes "the subjective existence of society thought and felt for itself."

The result of the technique of change, therefore, is a class-less and a state-less society. This is expressed as the "withering away of the state" in which a state is no longer necessary due to man's transformed nature. Now has arrived the dialectical synthesis; the parts are so related that individual claims to completeness are denied and yet aspects of each are maintained and ennobled in the inclusive whole. This is communism.

CHAPTER IV

SUMMARY AND EVALUATION

Within the pages of this book we have investigated the bearing of Marx's principle of activity on his materialism, his epistemology, and his conception of philosophy.

The specific element under discussion has been delineated as the PRINCIPLE of activity (rather than, for example, the idea of activity) because it is both a concept within Marx's theoretical system and a constituent of action illustrated in Marx's life. We have seen how the principle (as concept) influences the various parts of Marx's dialectical materialism. In each part of this philosophy it plays a significant and varying role. Likewise, we have seen how the principle (as constituent of action) is exemplified in Marx's own practice and the practice which he admonishes for his followers.

Now we shall summarize how the principle of activity affects and is related to various parts of Marx's system and evaluate Marx's ideas in detail.

In the body of the study it has been pointed out how Marx's entire philosophy is found within the larger context of his socio-economic theories. Marx's philosophy, that is, include sociological and economic theories. Philosophy, sociology, and economics are merged in the one system. There are few works by Marx which could be said to be pure philosophy, pure sociology, or pure economics. Even in *Capital* (predominantly dealing with economics) there are passages which are best defined as philosophical. What makes Marx's system unique, therefore, is that every philosophical concept has socio-economic foundation and reference. For example, labor for Marx is a basic part of his philosophy and also a primary term in his economics. This is the case with every key idea – it shares a many faceted base. This factor is significant in that it makes for concretization and the avoidance of needless abstraction in much of Marx's philosophy.

I. MATERIALISM

Marx was concerned to develop a new kind of materialism which should have an internal propelling force and avoid a mechanistic explanation of change and motion. Marx was thoroughly familiar with the earlier forms of materialism. In his doctoral dissertation he studied the materialism of Democritus and Epicurus. It was in Epicurus' concept of the declination (swerve) of the atoms that he found a partial answer to his problem. This "swaying" of the atoms in their downward path could serve as the basis for free motion within a materialistic schema.

Likewise, in Hegel's concept of dialectic as the motive force within his idealism, Marx discovered an idea which could serve in his materialism.

From Feuerbach, Marx took the conception of religious and philosophical ideas as the projection of human needs. The most significant aspect of life, Marx said, is man's means of livelihood – how he subsists. Man's physical (economic) needs are the foundation for all thought and action.

With such notions as these Marx forged the weapons of his arsenal. His materialism now contained an immanent principle which could explain and bring about a progressive pattern of development. This was the principle of dialectical *activity*.

2. EPISTEMOLOGY

Knowledge for Marx involves activity at both its poles – at the subject's end and the object's end. From his study of earlier forms of materialism, Marx saw that their explanation of knowledge had been in terms of material particles affecting a passive mind.

We have seen how in Marx the ontological reality of all entities is their activity. Subject and object have being insofar as they are active. From Kant, Marx took the idea of the active participation of the mind in knowledge. But whereas this action of the mind meant for Kant that we do not know reality, Marx averred that the mind's activity implies that we *do* know reality. Since the "empirical world" is in some sense man's active creation, then man can construct it in ways conducive to his own interest. Active participation in knowledge implies a grasp of reality.

If man draws all his knowledge, sensation, etc., from the world of the senses and the experience gained in it, the empirical world must be arranged so that in it man experiences and gets used to what is really human and that he becomes aware of himself as man.[1]

Thus, the object is active insofar as it is the cause of sensation. The subject is the active recipient and arranger of sensations out of which it makes its world. Marx's view of knowledge is the apprehension of the independently existing world which here assists in transforming reality. All true knowledge must end in action. Knowledge itself is not the material transformation of reality. Knowledge, however, is necessarily linked to such transformation. Ideas are not passive reflections of reality, they are active instruments of change.

Truth, Marx said, is tested by practice (*Praxis*). Ideas are proved true or false by using them to transform reality according to man's desire. Those ideas are true which assist in creating reality as predicted by the ideas themselves.

In our discussion we saw how Marx's epistemology and conception of truth have striking similarly with Dewey's instrumentalism.

3. PHILOSOPHY

In the concluding section of this study we gave attention to Marx's conception of philosophy. Philosophy as theory, said Marx, must be united with practice. Since man's being is his mode of activity, the most important practice is that of transforming society so as to allow for the fulfilment of man's powers. For Marx, society *is* the state – there is no separation in his system (as in Hegel's) between civil society and the state. We saw how Hegel's view of the state influenced Marx's conception.

In opposition to Hegel who saw the state as the embodiment of reason and freedom, Marx looked upon the state as the instrument of the ruling class used in exploiting and enslaving the working masses. Philosophy as criticism and theory is to assist in the transformation of society from capitalism to communism.

Philosophy's role is indeed a significant one in Marx's system. Marx condemned philosophy which is mere theory unrelated to material practice. Labeling his own type of philosophy "profane socialism," he said:

[1] K. Marx, *HF*, p. 31.

The first proposition of profane socialism rejects emancipation *in mere theory* as an illusion and for *real* freedom it demands besides the idealistic "will" quite palpable material conditions.[1]

This rejection of merely theoretical philosophy does not, however, mean that philosophy is negated by Marx (as some have contended). Marx and Engels were acutely aware of the significant role which philosophical theory plays in revolutionizing society. Philosophy is both descriptive and prescriptive. On the one hand it is a study of man's social relations. On the other hand the insights which it affords are used to predict and guide the active transformation of the existing order. We saw how this theory of philosophy can be significantly compared to Dewey's conception.

4. EVALUATION

Let us first consider the points of value in Marx's conception of the unity of theory and practice. Marx's view of philosophy as essentially related to practice is a much needed emphasis. Too often philosophy has been identified with an ivory tower kind of speculation. Philosophers themselves have assisted in giving this impression of their enterprise. They have made philosophy appear as a world apart.

Marx has the view that society's evolution can be directed by intelligent philosophic vision. Social theory must always be related to specific, practical problems. Philosophy must always relate itself to the practical affairs of changing the order of society.

There are several points in Marx's conception of the transformation of society which are unacceptable. He begins by assuming that the interest of the individual will merge into the interest of all by some sort of magic. Communistic society has never fulfilled all the promises which Marx made for it.

Marx's dialectic is both the highest value of his system and the greatest source of error. We have seen how the ideas upon which it is based have made a fine contribution to thought. But, in like manner, the employment of dialectic leads Marx to unfounded conceptions. First, the dialectic induces Marx to assume that the whole structure of present society must be wrong. Since there must be constant change the present forms *must be* in essential error. Real existence begins only in the synthesis stage; capitalism as the present structure *cannot* be conductive to truly human life.

[1] *Ibid.*, p. 27.

The answer to such a contention can only be a question: Why not? It must be proved, not merely assumed, that capitalism produces inhuman existence. This is not proved simply because the logic of the dialectic demands that the present forms be incorrect. Perhaps if Marx had looked more deeply into the basic concepts and practices underlying democratic capitalism he might have found elements which do in fact produce real life. Instead he is led astray by the impetus of the dialectic to say that capitalism can contain no right or truth because it is a present form and not the future synthesis.

The impetus of the dialectic was never fully dealt with by either Hegel or Marx. If the forward-moving action of the dialectic is a necessary element, then how can the process stop? How can the Prussian state of Hegel's day or the communistic society of Marx's vision be the end? If every synthesis becomes thesis for a following antithesis, and so on *ad infinitum*, there is no absolute or final conclusion. To choose some one form (either present or future) is to attempt to halt a necessarily unceasing movement.

A second error arises when Marx's dialectic prompts him to conceive of the necessity of a negating agency. If the dialectic is to have any motion and direction there must be a particular element of negativity. And to fill such a vacancy in the dialectical pattern Marx *chooses* the proletariat as the talismanic class. It appears evident that this is merely the arbitrary selection of a particular category (class). There is no stated principle of selection; just as with Hegel, the categories are chosen, with no further justification.

We must ask of Marx, then, why the proletariat is to be the instrument of dialectical movement. His answers are peculiarly vacuous. Since, says Marx, the proletariat marks the complete absence of the human essence it can serve to create a structure conducive to man's development. The proletariat gains this strange power, it would seem, because it receives no benefit from the existing class-structure and can, therefore, rise above it.

It is difficult to ferret out Marx's meaning here. If he is contending that the working-class will attack the existing order because it has nothing to lose, then there was a time (closer to his own day) when this was more true than today. In our age, the working masses have gained so many of the embellishments and comforts of life that they would have much to lose from a completely destructive revolution. If Marx is saying that the proletariat rises above the existing society in its desire for a new communal group, he is mistaken on two counts. First, working people do not have the time or the interest to spin fine theories of a socialized society; they remain in essential agreement with contemporary political and economic forms. Next, they continue to desire the products and rewards of the capitalist system no matter whether they receive them or not. Thus, in neither of these ways does the proletariat rise above present conditions.

The third element of inaccuracy is in regard to the synthesis-point of Marx's dialectic. Here the individual is merged into the whole. We would agree with the ideal of making the good of the whole the conscious end of the individual. But neither the methods of Hegel nor Marx are capable of bringing this about. It cannot be done by mere education which was Hegel's claim. For him the individual is progressively taught that his interests are integrally related to the interests of all by the experiences of life. Marx simply asserts that the interests of each will coincide with all – without explaining why or how. Communism, Marx asserts, assures the desired result.

Against both these positions we must offer a counter-opinion. Man does not accept the good of all as his good merely through education and experience. He can remain constant in his singularity no matter how often the lesson is foisted on him. And, likewise, individuality of desire still remains even in a so-called classless society. The contemporary forms of communist society are sufficient evidence of this. Individual and corporate end are merged only by the will of the individual. By his own free choice the person can incorporate into his life the desire to serve the ends of others. The form of society cannot create this; it can only make it possible. The final choice must be the individual's.

Another difficulty of this third area of the synthesis is in terms of the state itself. According to Marx this sphere can have no dominant agency. No government, as a repressive instrument, can be allowed. Contained within this idea is the naive assumption that communized men need no executive, legislative, or protective groups standing apart from them. Man, in communist society, suddenly becomes superhuman, able to discipline, lead, and legislate his existence by himself. We would argue (and give as evidence the present communist world) that man continually needs agencies that stand apart from him and over him. He needs such groups that will serve to restrict and lead him. There will continue to be the necessity of a government.

The last fallacy to which the dialectic disposes Marx is in seeing activity as the highest reality. Dialectical thought envisions process (activity) as the most real element within being. Particulars are parts of the ongoing whole; they can be demarcated only by the method of abstraction (as in Whitehead). The lines of division are never more than conceptual delineations; actually, each "entity" merges into every other in an inseparable, evolutionary process.

The being of the particular is his activity of becoming and passing away. Man, Marx says, is created by his activity of objectification in labor. Through his toil the human person creates both himself and his world. Labor as the creative activity, therefore, becomes more real than man. Man is a derivative of act.

Since labor is social, society (the relation between creative acts) is also of a higher reality than man. With such a foundation Marx finds it easy to posit communism as the structure which creates human life. Individuals gain significance and reality insofar as they are members of the communist state, just as individuals gain their meaning for Hegel by being parts of the Absolute.

Marx criticized Hegel for making logic most real; he criticized Feuerbach for constructing only an abstract man. But Marx's "socialized man" is just as unreal and abstract as those two earlier views. Man, for Marx, remains a second-class reality, derived from pure act and given meaning only by his membership within communism.

Our final evaluation of Marx is in relation to his conception of the role of philosophy. One of the most significant of Marx's contributions to modern thought is his view of philosophy as essentially related to practice.

A study of Marx's life convinces one that as a philosopher he actively entered into important events in his own day. He not only worked out in theory but illustrated in practice what should be the role of the philosopher in society. Marx entered into dynamic debate with many of the finest minds of his era. Philosophy (and all of modern life) today has altogether too little of this element of informed disagreement. It is as if the successors of Socrates and Plato had suddenly reached a gentlemen's agreement not to disagree. "If you will not criticize me, I shall not criticize you and we'll all have a jolly time of it." "Let us agree to be agreeable." These seem to express the common sentiment. Why this unanimity of opinion? Perhaps it is because we do not study issues sufficiently to be able to argue intelligently about them. Perhaps there is the underlying fear that were someone to examine another's ideas we would find a storehouse of nothingness, a paucity of knowledge, a citadel of confusion.

The keynote of the philosophic adventure of this day appears to be:

Appreciation. The first rule of pedagogy becomes – learn to see the good in every philosopher, every philosophic system. Each school is to be given its fair "shake" no matter what its outcome or its relation to life. This is carried over, of course, into our common existence in the form of the necessity of allowing and "appreciating" every wind of doctrine and every expression of opinion. What does it matter that a man's philosophy is in essential error? What conceivable difference could it make that a philosophic system has led to destructive results?

We are not advocating the blind rejection of a theory because it has produced damnable results. It is the first responsibility of a critic to understand the object of his assessment. To this, almost all would agree – the necessity of careful study. But it is the consequent adjudicating, estimating and concluding which are so heartily denounced today.

The tendencies noted above give partial answer to why scholars are so often parodied as a group of gentle, harmless fools. The proper inspection and review of a position is necessary; but what must follow this, if scholarship is once again to be of significance, is the making of a decision, the settling of an opinion, the acting upon conviction.

Marx, in his own practice, showed how philosophy can and should involve itself in discussion and controversy. His criticisms of other men were well-conceived and thoughtful. He dared to come to a decisive position regarding the thought of other men. Such precision gave his own philosophy the basic clarity necessary for its instrumentality in the transformation of society.

Marxism is one of the best examples of a philosophic system which became the basis for economic and political practice. Its influence as a system is so widespread as to be almost beyond conception. Today, more knees bow to the name of Marx than to any other man.

If philosophy is to become a conscious partner with practice in bringing about a more ideal society, then the methods which Marx employed will be considered with good advantage. Certainly the specific facets of dialectical materialism will be repudiated as false (as shown by communist practice), but Marx's method of uniting philosophy and practice will serve as a worthy example to future ages.

BIBLIOGRAPHY

Marx, K., *Marx-Engels, Historisch-kritische Gesamtausgabe*, edited by D. Rjazanov. 9 vols. Frankfurt, 1927–1932.

—, *Aus dem literarischen Nachlass von Karl Marx, Friedrich Engels*, edited by F. Mehring. 3. vols. Stuttgart, 1902.

—, *A Contribution to the Critique of Political Economy*. New York: Inter. Pub., 1904.

—, *Capital* (tr. by Eden and Cedar Paul). 2 vols. London: Dent and Sons, 1930.

—, *Economic and Philosophic Manuscripts of 1844* (tr. by M. Milligan). Foreign Lang. Pub. House, 1960.

—, *Selected Works*. New York: Inter. Pub., 2 vols, no date.

—, *The Communist Manifesto*. New York: Inter. Pub., 1935.

—, *The German Ideology*. New York: Inter. Pub., 1939.

—, *The Holy Family*. Moscow: Foreign Lang. Pub. House, 1956.

—, *The Poverty of Philosophy*. Chicago: C. H. Kerr, 1913.

Adams, H. P., *Karl Marx in his Earlier Writings*. London: Allen and Unwin, 1940.

Adoratsky, V., *Dialectical Materialism*. London: M. Lawrence, 1934.

Beer, M., *The Life and Teachings of Marx*. London: Parsons Co., 1921.

—, *A Guide to the Study of Marx*. London: Labor Research Dept., 1923.

Bober, M., *Karl Marx's Interpretion of History*. Cambridge: Harvard Univ. Press, 1927.

Bohm-Bawerk, E., *Karl Marx and the Close of His System*. London: T Union Co., 1898.

Boudin, L., *The Theoretical System of Karl Marx*. Chicago: C. H. Kerr, 1907.

* Brameld, T., *A Philosophic Approach to Communism*. Chicago: Univ. of Chicago Press, 1933.

Bukharin, N., *The A B C of Communism*. London: Communist Party Press, 1922.

—, *Historical Materialism*. New York: Inter. Pub., 1925.

—, *Marxism and Modern Thought*. New York: Harcourt-Brace, 1935.

Burns, E., *A Handbook of Marxism*. London: Gollancz, 1935.

Carritt, E. F., "Discussion: Hegel and Prussianism," *Philosophy*, 15: 191–194.

* Chang, S., *The Marxian Theory of the State*. Phila.: Univ. of Penn. Press, 1931.

Cole, G., *What Marx Really Means*. New York: A. A. Knopf, 1934.

Collins, J., *The Existentialists*. Chicago: Regnery, 1952.

Conze, E., *Dialectical Materialism*. London: N.C.L.C. Soc., 1936.

Note: The following bibliography largely contains books and articles cited in the preceding pages. For general bibliographies of Marx's works see the titles marked with an asterisk.

Cooper, R., *The Logical Influence of Hegel on Marx.* Seattle: Wash. Univ. Press, 1925.
Cornforth, M., *In Defense of Philosophy.* New York: Int. Pub., 1950.
Croce, B., *Historical Materialism and the Economics of Marx.* New York: Macmillan, 1914.
Dewey, J., *A Common Faith.* New Haven: Yale Univ. Press, 1934.
—, *Creative Intelligence.* New York: Holt, 1917.
—, *Essays in Experimental Logic.* New York: Dover, 1953.
—, *Experience and Nature.* New York: Dover Publications, 1958.
—, *The Influence of Darwin on Philosophy.* New York: Holt, 1910.
—, *The Quest for Certainty.* New York: Minton, Balch, 1929.
Dunayevskaya, R., *Marxism and Freedom.* New York: Bookman Ass., 1958.
Eastman, M., *Marx, Lenin, and the Science of Revolution.* London: Allen and Unwin, 1926.
Engels, F., *Ludwig Feuerbach.* New York: Int. Publ., 1934.
—, *Socialism: Utopian and Scientific.* New York: Int. Publ., 1935.
Feuerbach, L. A., *The Essence of Christianity.* Boston: Houghton-Mifflin. 1881.
Foster, M. B., *The Political Philosophies of Plato and Hegel,* Oxford: Clarendon Press, 1935.
Greene, T. M. (ed.), *Kant Selections.* New York: Scribners Sons, 1929.
Hegel, J. W. F., *The Logic of Hegel* (Wallace). Oxford, 1892.
—, *Reason in History.* New York: Lib. Arts Press, 1953.
—, *The Phenomenology of Mind* (Baillie). London: Sonnenschein, 1910.
—, *The Philosophy of Right* (Knox). Oxford, 1942.
Hook, S., *From Hegel to Marx.* New York: John Day, 1936.
—, *Reason, Social Myths and Democracy.* New York: John Day, 1940.
—, *Towards an Understanding of Karl Marx.* New York: John Day, 1933.
Jackson, T., *Dialectics: The Logic of Marxism.* London: Lawrence, 1936.
Joad, C. E. M., *A Guide to Philosophy.* New York: Dover, 1936.
Jones, W. T., *A History of Western Philosophy.* New York: Harcourt, 1952.
Knox, T. M., "Hegel and Prussianism," *Philosophy,* 15, 1940.
Lawrence, C., "Roots of the Marxist Concept of Practice," *Science and Society,* 13: 229–242.
Lenin, V., *Materialism and Empirio-Criticism.* New York, Int. Publ., 1927.
Lowith, K., "Man's Self- Alienation in the Early Writings of Marx," *Social Research,* 21, 1954.
Macintyre, A. C., *Marxism, An Interpretation.* London: SCM Press, 1953.
Macmurray, J., *The Philosophy of Communism.* London: Faber, 1933.
—, *The Self as Agent.* New York: Harper, 1957.
Marcel, G., *The Decline of Wisdom.* New York: Phil. Lib., 1955.
Marcuse, H., *Reason and Revolution.* London: Oxford, 1941.
Mayo, H.B., *An Introduction to Marxist Theory.* New York: Oxford, 1960.
—, *Democracy and Marxism.* New York: Oxford, 1955.
McCoy, C. N. R., "Ludwig Feuerbach and the Formation of the Marxian Revolutionary Idea," *Théologique et Philosophique,* 7, 1951.
McFadden, C. J., *The Philosophy of Communism.* Nwe York: Benziger, 1939.
Mehring, F., *Karl Marx,* London: John Lane, 1936.
—, "La These de Karl Marx Sur Democrite et Epicure," *La Nouvelle Critique,* 61, 1955.
Mins, H. F., "Marx' Doctoral Dissertation," *Science and Society,* 12, 1948.
Montague, W. P., *The Ways of Knowing.* London: Unwin and Allen, 1928.
Morris, G. S., *Hegel's Philosophy of the State and of History.* Chicago: Scott, Foresman and Co., 1902.

Plakhanov, G., *Essays in the History of Materialism*. London: John Lane, 1934.
Popper, K. R., *The Open Society and Its Enemies*. Princeton, 1950.
Reyburn, H. A., *The Ethical Theory of Hegel*. London: Oxford, 1921.
Rjazanov, D., *Marx-Engels-Archiv*. Frankfurt: V.M.V.H., no date.
* Rubel, M., *Bibliographie des Oeuvres de Karl Marx*. Paris: Librairie Marcel Rivière et Cie, 1956.
Seth, A., *Hegelianism and Personality*. London: Blackwood and Sons. 1893.
Spinoza, B., *Ethics*. New York: Hafner, 1949.
Stace, W. T., *The Philosophy of Hegel*. London: Macmillan, 1924.
Thalheimer, A., *Dialectical Materialism*. New York: Covici-Friede, 1936.
Venable, V., *Human Nature: The Marxian View*. New York: A. A. Knopf, 1945.
Voegelin, E., "The Formation of the Marxian Revolutionary Idea," *Revirw of Politics*. 12, 1950.
Wetter, G. A., *Dialectical Materialism*. New York: Praeger, 1958.

AN ENGLISH TRANSLATION OF MARX'S DOCTORAL DISSERTATION

THE DIFFERENCE BETWEEN THE DEMOCRITEAN AND EPICUREAN PHILOSOPHY OF NATURE

WITH AN APPENDIX

by

KARL HEINRICH MARX, PH. D.

To his dear fatherly friend,
Ludwig von Weshphalen, Privy Councillor at Trier,
the author dedicates these lines as a token of filial love.

You will forgive me, my dear fatherly friend, if I set your name, so dear to me, at the head of an insignificant brochure. I am too impatient to await another opportunity of showing you a small proof of my love.

May everyone who despairs of the Idea be so fortunate as I, to be able to admire an old man with the strength of youth, who greets every forward step of the times with the enthusiasm and the prudence of truth and with that sun-bright idealism, deep with conviction, which alone knows the true word before which all the spirits of the world appear, which never recoils before the deep shadows of retrograde ghosts, before the often dark clouds of the times, but rather with divine energy and a certain, manly gaze looks through all veils to see the *empyreum* which burns at the heart of the world. You, my father friend, were always a living *argumentum ad oculos* to me, that idealism is no figment of the imagination, but a truth.

I need not pray for physical well-being for you. The spirit is the great physician versed in magic, to whom you have trusted yourself.

FOREWORD

The form of this treatise would have been on the one hand more strictly scientific, on the other hand in many of its arguments less pedantic, if its primary purpose had not been that of a doctoral dissertation. I am nevertheless constrained by external reasons to send it to the press in this form. Moreover I believe I have solved in it a heretofore unsolved problem in the history of Greek philosophy.

The experts know that no even remotely usable preliminary studies exist for the subject of this treatise. What Cicero and Plutarch have prated has been prated after them up to the present day. Gassendi, who freed Epicurus from the interdict which the fathers of the Church and the whole Middle Ages, the period of consuumate unreason had placed upon him, presents in his expositions only one interesting element. He seeks to accomodate his Catholic conscience with his pagan knowledge and Epicurus with the Church, which was certainly wasted effort. It is as though one tried to throw the vestment of a Christian nun over the splendid and flourishing body of a Greek layman. It is more correct to say that Gassendi learns philosophy from Epicurus than that he enlightens us about Epicurus' philosophy.

This treatise is to be regarded as only the preliminary to a larger essay, in which I will present in detail the cycle of Epicurean, Stoic and Sceptical philosophy in relation to all Greek Speculation. The failings of this treatise, in form and the like, will be corrected in that work.

To be sure, Hegel has correctly defined the general aspects of the above-mentioned systems as a whole. But in the admirably great and bold plan of his history of philosophy, which must indeed be regarded as the beginning of the history of philosophy, it was in some way impossible to go into detail, and in some way the gigantic thinker was hindered by his view of what he called the speculative idea *par excellence* from recognizing in these systems the great importance that they have for the history of Greek philosophy and for the Greek mind in general.

These systems are the key to the true history of Greek philosophy. Concerning their connection with Greek life there is a more profound suggestion in the essay of my friend Koppen, *Friedrich der Grosse und seine Widersacher*.

If as an appendix a critique of Plutarch's polemic against Epicurus' theology has been added, this is because this polemic is by no means isolated, but rather representative of a species, in that in itself it most strikingly presents the relation of the theologizing intellect to philosophy.

Among other things I shall not discuss in the critique how false Plutarch's standpoint is when he brings philosophy before the forum of religion. It will be enough to cite, in place of all argument, a passage from David Hume:

> It is certainly a kind of insult to philosophy, whose sovereign authority ought to be acknowledged on all sides, if one forces it to defend itself on every occasion because of its conclusions and to justify itself against every art and science that takes offense at it. One thinks of a king accused of high treason against his own subjects.

Philosophy, as long as a drop of blood shall beat in its heart, being absolutely free and master of the universe, will never grow tired of throwing to its adversaries the cry of Epicurus: "The blasphemous is not he who scorns the gods of the masses, but those who adhere to the idea that the masses create the gods."

Philosophy does not make a secret of it. The profession of Prometheus: "In simple words, I hate the pack of gods," is its own profession, its own aphorism against all divine and earthly gods who do not acknowledge human self-consciousness as the highest divinity. It allows no rivals.

But to those poor March hares, who rejoice over the apparently worsened social position of philosophy, it responds again, as Prometheus replied to the servant of the gods, Hermes:

> Be sure of this, I would not change my state
> Of evil fortune for your servitude.
> Better to be the servant of this rock
> Than to be faithful boy to Father Zeus.

Prometheus is the most eminent saint and martyr in the philosophic calendar.

Berlin, March 1841

PART ONE *

THE DIFFERENCE BETWEEN THE DEMOCRITEAN AND EPICUREAN PHILOSOPHY OF NATURE IN GENERAL

I. THE SUBJECT OF THE TREATISE

What should not occur in a good tragedy seems to happen to Greek philosophy: a weak ending. The objective history of philosophy in Greece seems to end with Aristotle, the Macedonian Alexander of Greek philosophy, and even the manly Stoics do not seem to succeed, as the Spartans in their temples succeeded in binding Hercules to Athena so that she could not fly away.

Epicureans, Stoics and Sceptics are regarded as an almost improper postcript to Aristotelianism, having no relation to powerful premises. Epicurean philosophy is taken as a syncretistic combination of Democritean physics and Cyrenaic morality; Stoicism as a compendium of Heraclitic nature speculation, Cynical ethical world-view and perhaps also Aristotelian logic; and finally Scepticism as the necessary evil which opposes these dogmatisms. One unconsciously links these philosophies to Alexandrian philosophy in making of them a narrow and tendentious eclecticism. Finally, Alexandrian philosophy is regarded as complete fanaticism and ruin – a confusion in which at most the universality of intention can be recognized.

Now it is, to be sure, a trivial truism that birth, development and death constitute the brazen cycle in which everything human is caught up, through which everything must pass. So it is not surprising if Greek philosophy, after reaching its zenith in Aristotle, should then have withered. But the death of a hero resembles the setting of the sun, not the bursting of a frog which has blown itself up.

And further: birth, development and death are very general, very vague ideas, in which certainly everything can be included, but through

* In the footnotes I have tried to assist the reader as much as possible by: (a) Giving English translations of long Greek or Latin passages when available; (b) Wherever possible giving a more recent citation where the original reference is outdated; (c) Reproducing the original notes when translations or more recent citations are not available.

which nothing is to be comprehended. Death itself is prefigured in the living thing; its form is therefore to be grasped equally in its specific individual character just as is the form of life.

Finally, if we take a glance at history, are Epicureanism, Stoicism and Scepticism special phenomena? Are they not rather prototypes of the Roman mind, the form in which Greece emigrated to Rome? Are they not such intense and eternal beings, so full of character, that even the modern world has to allow to them their full spiritual citizenship?

I lay stress on this only to call to mind the historical importance of these systems. Here, however, we are not dealing with their general importance for the history of civilization, here we are dealing with their relation to previous Greek philosophy.

Should not this relation incite us to research, seeing that Greek philosophy finishes with two different groups of eclectic systems, one of which constitutes the cycle of Epicurean, Stoic and Sceptic philosophies, the other of which is known under the title of Alexandrian philosophy? Furthermore, is it not remarkable that after the Platonic and Aristotelian philosophies, which extend to universality, new systems appear which do not refer back to these rich intellectual figures, but, looking farther back, turn to the simplest schools – in regard to physics, to the philosophers of nature, in regard to ethics, to the Socratic school? Further still, what is the basis for the fact that the systems that follow after Aristotle find their foundations more or less laid in the past so that we relate Democritus to the Cyrenaics and Heraclitus to the Cynics? Is it an accident that with the Epicureans, Stoics and Sceptics all the elements of self-consciousness are represented as complete, except that each element is represented as a particular existence? Is it an accident that these systems taken together form the complete structure of self-consciousness? Finally, consider the character with which Greek philosophy mythically begins in the seven sages, which, just as its center point is embodied in Socrates as the demiurge, I mean the character of the sage – of the *sophos* – is it an accident that it is put forth in those systems as the reality of true science?

It seems to me that if the preceding systems are more significant and more interesting because of their content, the post-Aristotelian ones, and particularly the cycle of Epicurean, Stoic and Sceptic schools are important because of the subjective form, the character of Greek philosophy. It is precisely the subjective form, the spiritual carrier of philosophical systems, which we have until now almost entirely ignored in considering only their metaphysical pronouncements.

I shall save for a more exhaustive discussion the presentation of Epicurean, Stoic and Sceptical philosophy in their totality and in their total relationship to earlier and later Greek philosophy.

Here it is sufficient to illustrate this relationship with a single example, and develop only one aspect of it, namely, its relation to earlier speculation.

As such an example I select the relationship of the Epicurean to the Democritean philosophy of nature. I do not believe that it is the simplest point of contact. Because on the one hand it is a well-established prejudice to identify Democritean and Epicurean physics, so that people see in Epicurus' modifications only arbitrary ideas. On the other hand I am forced to go into detail concerning phenomenal atomistics. But precisely because this prejudice is as old as the history of philosophy, because the differences are so concealed that they can be found as it were only with a microscope, the result will be all the more important if, despite the relation between the Democritean and the Epicurean physics, an essential difference extending to the smallest detail can be demonstrated. What can be demonstrated on a small scale can be demonstrated even more easily where the relationships are understood in larger dimensions, while conversely completely general discussions leave doubt whether the result will hold good when applied to the details.

II. JUDGMENTS CONCERNING THE RELATIONSHIP OF DEMOCRITEAN AND EPICUREAN PHYSICS

How my view relates in general to earlier ones will become instantly clear if we quickly pass in review the judgments of the ancients concerning the relationship of Democritean and Epicurean physics.

Posidonius the Stoic, Nicholas and Sotion reproach Epicurus for having presented the Democritean doctrine of atoms and Aristippus' teaching on pleasure as his own.[1] Cotta the Academician asks in Cicero: "What is there in Epicurus' physics which does not belong to Democritus? Of course he modifies some details, but most of it he simply repeats from him." [2] So says Cicero himself: "In physics, where he is

[1] Diogen. Laert. X, 2. They are followed by Posidorius the Stoic and his school, and Nicolaus and Sotion that he (Epicurus) put forward as his own ... the doctrines of Democritus about atoms and of Aristippus about pleasure.

[2] Cic. de Nat. Deor. I, 26. What is there in Epicurus' natural philosophy that does not come from Democritus? Since even if he introduced some alterations ... yet most of his system is the same.

the most pretentious, Epicurus is a perfect layman. Most of it belongs to Democritus; where he deviates from him, where he endeavors to improve, he spoils and worsens it." [1] Although many authors reproach Epicurus for aspersions against Democritus, nonetheless Leonteus, according to Plutarch, claims that Epicurus honored Democritus because the latter had professed the true doctrine before him and had previously discovered the principles of nature.[2] In the essay *De placitis philosophorum*, Epicurus is said to have created his philosophy from Democritus.[3] Plutarch in his *Adversus Coloten* goes farther. Successively comparing Epicurus with Democritus, Empedocles, Parmenides, Plato, Socrates, Stilpon, the Cyrenaics and the Academicians, he endeavors to prove that: "Epicurus appropriated from Greek philosohy only the false and did not understand the true." [4] And the treatise *De eo, quod secundum Epicurum non beate vivi possit* teems with malevolent insinuations of a similar kind.

This unfavorable opinion of older writers is found again in the Church fathers. In the notes I cite only one passage from Clement of Alexandria,[5] a Church father who with regard to Epicurus deserves prominent mention, because he re-interprets St. Paul's warning against philosophy in general into a warning against Epicurean philosophy under the pretext that the latter had not even introduced providence and the like into his speculation.[6] But the tendency that people have in general of accusing Epicurus of plagiarism appears in the most striking manner in Sextus Empiricus who wished to make some absolutely unsatisfactory passages of Homer and Epicharme the principal sources of Epicurean philosophy.[7]

It is well known that modern writers by and large make Epicurus a mere plagiarist of Democritus in regard to the philosophy of nature. The following statement of Leibniz can here represent their opinion in

[1] Id. de Fin. I, 6. His doctrines are those of Democritus, with a very few modifications. Ib. Let me begin with the subject of Natural philosophy, which is Epicurus' particular boast. Here ,in the first place, he is entirely second-hand. His doctrines are those of Democritus, with a few modifications. And as for the latter, where he attempts to improve upon his original, in my opinion he only succeeds in making things worse.

[2] Plutarch. Colot.

[3] Id. de Placit. Philos.

[4] Id. Colot.

[5] Clemens Alex. Strom. VI. (Marx's note refers to an edition no longer in print making it impossible to determine the location of the passage. This work is translated into English in *The Ante-Nicene Fathers*, Vol. II, Scribners, N.Y., 1899.)

[6] Id.

[7] Sext. Empir. adv. Math. (This work is now translated into English in the Loeb Library. Marx's note refers to an edition no longer in print making it impossible to determine the location of the passage.)

general: "Of this great man (Democritus) we scarcely know what Epicurus has borrowed from him, who was not capable of always taking the best." [1]

Thus while Cicero claims that Epicurus spoiled the Democritean doctrine but at least grants him the intention to improve it and the faculty of seeing its defects; while Plutarch ascribes to him inconsistency[2] and a predetermined inclination toward the worst, i.e., casts suspicion on his intention as well; Leibniz denies him even the capacity of taking excerpts from Democritus competently.

But all agree that Epicurus borrowed his physics from Democritus.

III. DIFFICULTIES WITH REGARD TO THE IDENTITY OF THE DEMOCRITEAN AND EPICUREAN PHILOSOPHY OF NATURE

Aside from the historical testimony, much else speaks for the identity of Democritean and Epicurean physics. The principle elements – atoms and the void – are undeniably the same. Only in individual statements does there seem to be an arbitrary, therefore unessential, difference.

But there remains a riddle which cannot be solved. Two philosophers teach exactly the same science, in exactly the same way but – how inconsistent! – they stand diametrically opposed in all that regards truth, certainty, the application of this science, in all that regards the relationship of thought and reality in general. I say they stand diametrically opposed, and I will now try to prove this.

(A) Democritus' opinion concerning the truth and certainty of human knowledge seems difficult to ascertain. There are contradictory passages, or rather it is not the passages but Democritus' views that contradict each other. Trendelenburg's claim in his commentary to Aristotelian psychology, that only later writers, but not Aristotle, knew of such contradiction, is factually incorrect. In Aristotle's psychology it says namely: "Democritus sets up the feeling (*Seele*) and the understanding (*Verstand*) as one and the same, because the phenomenon is the true." [3] But in the *Metaphysics*, he says: "Democritus says that either there is no truth or we cannot discover it." [4] Are not these pas-

[1] Lettres de Leibnitz à Mr. des Maizeaux, contenant éclaircissements sur l'explication etc.

[2] Plutarch. Colot.

[3] Aristot. de Anima. I.

[4] Id. Metaph. IV, 5. And hence Democritus says that either there is no truth or we cannot discover it. And in general it is because they suppose that thought is sense-perception, and snese-perception physical alteration, that they say that the impression given through sense-

sages from Aristotle contradictory? If the phenomenon is the true, how can the true be hidden? The fact of being hidden begins at the moment when the phenomenon and the truth are separated. But Diogenes Laertius reports that people counted Democritus among the Sceptics. His aphorism is cited: "In truth we know nothing, because the truth lies at the unfathomable bottom of the well." [1] Similar affirmations are to be found in Sextus Empiricus.[2]

This sceptical, uncertain and internally contradictory view of Democritus is only further developed in the way in which the relationship of the atom and the sensible world is determined.

On the one hand sensible appearance is not ascribed to the atoms themselves. It is not a question of objective appearance, but subjective illusion. "The true principle elements (*Prinzipien*) are the atoms and the void; everything else is opinion, illusion."[3] Only according to opinion is there cold, only according to opinion heat, but in truth there are only atoms and the void." [4] Consequently in truth unity does not come out of the many atoms, but rather "through the combination of atoms each thing seems to be one." [5] Therefore the principle elements are only to be considered through reason, as they are already inaccessible to the sensible eye because of their smallness, they are thus called ideas.[6] On the other hand the sensible appearance is the only true object, and the *aisthēsis* is the *phronēsis*, the true however is changing, unstable phenomenon. To say that the phenomenon is the true is contradictory.[7] First the one side then the other is made the subjective and the objective. Thus the contradiction seems dissipated in that it is divided between two worlds. Consequently, Democritus makes sensible reality subjective illusion; but the antinomy, banned from the world of objects, exists now in his own self-consciousness, where the concept of the atom and the sensible perception meet as enemies.

Thus Democritus does not escape the antinomy. This is not the place to explain it. It is enough that we cannot deny its existence.

perception is necessarily true; for it is on these grounds that both Empedocles and Democritus and practically all the rest have become obsessed by such opinions as these.

[1] Diogen. Laert. IX, 72. Furthermore, they find Xenophanes, Zeno of Elea, and Democritus to be sceptics: ... Democritus [says] ... of a truth we know nothing, for truth is in a well.

[2] Cf. Ritter's Gesch. d. alt. Philos. I.

[3] Diogen. Laert. IX, 44. His (Democritus') opinions are these. The first principles of the universe are atoms and empty space; everything else is merely thought to exist.

[4] Id. ib. 72. Democritus: "Opinion says hot or cold, but the reality is atoms and empty space ..."

[5] Simplic. in Schol. ad Aristot.

[7] Plutarch. Colot.

[7] Cf. Aristot. 1. c.

On the other hand let us listen to Epicurus. "The sage," he says, "takes a dogmatic, not a sceptical position." [1] Yes, just that is his advantage over everybody, that he knows with conviction.[2] "All the senses are heralds of the true." [3] "Nothing can refute sensible perception; neither can like refute like because of their equal validity, nor can unlike refute unlike, because they do not pass judgment on the same thing, nor the concept, because the concept depends upon sensible perception," [4] as it says in *The Canon*. While Democritus reduces the sensible world to subjective illusion, Epicurus reduces it to objective appearance. And he makes a conscious differentiation here, for he admits that he shares the same principles, but does not turn sensible qualities into something which is only the result of opinion.[5]

Then if sensible perception was in fact Epicurus' criterion, if the objective appearance corresponds to it, then one can only regard as a correct conclusion that at which Cicero shrugs his shoulders: "The sun seems large to Democritus because he is a scientist trained in geometry; to Epicurus it seems to be about two feet in diameter because he claims it *is* as large as it *seems*." [6]

(B) This difference in the theoretical judgments of Democritus and Epicurus about the certainty of science and the truth of their objects manifests itself in the disparate scientific energy and practice of these men.

Democritus, for whom the principle element does not enter appearance and remains without reality and existence, is on the other hand faced with the world of sensible perception as a real and concrete world. This world is, to be sure, subjective illusion, but just because of this it is torn free from the principle element, left in its autonomous reality; at the same time it is the unique, real object and as such has value and importance. Democritus is consequently driven to empirical observation. Dissatisfied with philosophy, he throws himself into the arms of positive knowledge. We have already seen that Cicero calls him a *vir*

[1] Diogen. Laert. X, 121. He will be a dogmatist but not a mere sceptic.

[2] Plutarch. Colot.

[3] Cic. de Nat. Deor. I, 25.
Cf. Id. de Fin. I, 4.
(Plutarch.) de Placit. Philos. IV.

[4] Diogen. Laert. X, 31. Now in the *Canon* Epicurus affirms that our sensations and preconceptions and our feelings are the standards of truth; ... Nor is there anything which can refute sensations or convict them of error: one sensation cannot convict another and kindred sensation, for they are equally valid; not can one sensation refute another which is not kindred but heterogeneous, for the objects which the two senses judge are not the same ...

[5] Plutarch. Colot. l. c.

[6] Cic. de Fin. I, 6. Cf. (Plutarch.) de Placit. Philos. II

eruditus. He is competent in physics, ethics, mathematics, in the encyclopedic disciplines, in every art.[1] Even the catalogue of his books given by Diogenes Laertius bears witness to his erudition.[2] As erudition has the characteristic of extending in breadth and collecting and observing afar, so we see Democritus travelling through half the world in order to exchange experiences, pieces of knowledge and observations. "Of all my contemporaries," he claims, "I have wandered over the largest portion of the earth, investigating the most remote things; and I have seen the majority of climates and lands, and I have heard the greatest men of learning, and in linear composition with figures no one surpassed me, not even the so-called Arsipedonaptes of the Egyptians."[3]

Demetrius in the *homonumois* and Antisthenes in the *diadochais* report that he travelled to Egypt to the priests in order to learn geometry, and to the Chaldeans in Persia, and that he went as far as the Red Sea. Some claim he also met the Gymnosophists in India and visited Ethiopia.[4] On the one hand it is the lust for knowledge that leaves him no peace, but it is at the same time the dissatisfaction with the true, i.e. philosophical knowledge that drives him afar. The knowledge which he considers true is contentless; the knowledge that gives it content is without truth. It could be a fable, but it is a true fable because this anecdote of the ancients describes the contradiction in his being. Democritus is supposed to have blinded himself so that the sensible light in the eye would not darken sharpness of intellect.[5] This is the same man who, according to Cicero, travelled through the whole world. But he did not find what he was seeking.

In Epicurus an opposite figure appears to us.

Epicurus is satisfied and blissful in philosophy. "You must," he says, "serve philosophy so that true freedom will be your lot. He who subordinates himself and gives himself over to it does not need to wait; he is immediately emancipated. For to serve philosophy is freedom it-

[1] Diogen. Laert. IX, 37. And truly Democritus was versed in every department of philosophy, for he had trained himself both in physics and in ethics, nay more, in mathematics and the routine subject of education, and he was quite an expert in the arts.

[2] Cf. Diogen. Laert. IX, 46 seq.

[3] Euseb. Praepar. evang, X.

[4] Diogen. Laert. IX. 35. According to Demetrius in his book on *Men of the Same Name* and Aristhenes in his *Successions of Philosophers*, he (Democritus) travelled into Egypt to learn geometry from the priests, and he also went into Persia to visit the Chaldeans as well as to the Red Sea. Some say that he associated with the Gymnosophists in India and went to Aethiopia.

[5] Cic. Quaest. Tusc. V, 39. Id. de Fin. V, 29.

self." [1] Consequently he teaches: "Neither let the youth hesitate to philosophize nor let the old man desist from philosophy. For none is too young, none too mature, to gain healing for his soul. But he who says either that time for philosophizing has not yet come or that it is past, is like a person who maintains that the hour for happiness has not yet come or is no more." [2] While Democritus, dissatisfied with philosophy, throws himself into the arms of empirical knowledge, Epicurus scorns the positive sciences because in his opinion they contribute nothing to true perfection.[3] He is called an enemy of science, a scorner of grammar. [4] He is accused of ignorance itself; "but," says an Epicurean in Cicero, "it is not Epicurus who lacks erudition, but they are ignorant who believe that what is shameful for a boy not to know ought also to be still recited by the old man."[5]

But while Democritus seeks to learn from Egyptian priests, Persian Chaldeans and Indian Gymnosophists, Epicurus prides himself for not having had a teacher, for being self-taught.[6] Some people, he says, quoting Seneca, pursue truth without the least assistance. It is in the ranks of the latter that he traced out his path for himself. And it is for these, the self-taught, that he has the greatest praise. The others, to believe him, are second-class intellects.[7] While Democritus is driven into all parts of the world, Epicurus leaves his garden in Athens scarcely two or three times to travel to Ionia, not to give himself to studies but to visit friends.[8] While finally Democritus, despairing of knowledge, blinds himself, Epicurus, feeling the hour of his death coming, takes a

[1] Luc. Ann. Senec. Op. II. epist. i, 0.24.

[2] Diogen. Leart. X, 122. Let no one be slow to seek wisdom when he is young nor weary in the search thereof when he is grown old. For no age is too early or too late for the health of the soul. And to say that the season for studying philosophy has not yet come or that it is past and gone is like saying that the season for happiness is not yet or that it is now no more. Therefore, both old and young ought to seek wisdom, the former in order that, as age comes over him, he may be young in good things because of the grace of what has been, and the latter in order that, while he is young, he may at the same time be old, because he has no fear of the things which are to come. Cf. Clemens. Alex. IV.

[3] Sext. Emp. adv. Math. The case against the professors of arts and sciences has been set forth in a general way, it would seem, both by Epicurus and by the School of Pyrrho, although the standpoints they adopt are different. Epicurus took the ground that the subjects taught are of no help in perfecting wisdom.

[4] Id. Id. Cf. Plutarch.

[5] Cic. de Fin. I, 21.

[6] Diogen. Laert. X, 13. Cic. de Nat. Deor. I, 26.

[7] Senec. Epist. 52.

[8] Diogen. Laert. X, 10. He spent all his life in Greece, notwithstanding the calamities which had befallen her in that age; when he did once or twice take a trip to Ionia, it was to visit friends there. Friends indeed came to him from all parts and lived with him in his garden. This is stated by Apollodorus, who also says that he purchased the garden for eighty minae.

warm bath and calls for pure wine and recommends to his friends that they remain faithful to philosophy.[1]

(C) The differences just adumbrated are not to be ascribed to the accidental individuality of the two philosophers; they are two opposing tendencies which materialize here. We see as a difference in practical energy that which expresses itself above as a difference in the theoretical consciousness.

We consider finally the form of reflection, which expresses the relation of thought to being in their reciprocal relation. In the general relationship which the philosopher establishes between the world and thought, he merely makes objective the relation between his particular consciousness and the real world.

Now Democritus uses necessity as a form of reflection of reality.[2] Aristotle says of him that he reduces everything to necessity.[3] Diogenes Laertius reports that the vortex of atoms, the origin of all, is the Democritean necessity.[4] More satisfying explanations are furnished by the author of *De placitis philosophorum*: necessity is, according to Democritus, fate and law, the providence and creator of the world. But the substance of this necessity is the antitype, the movement and impulse of matter.[5] A similar passage is to be found in the *Physical Eclogues* of Stabaeus [6] and in the sixth book of the *Praeparatio evangelica* of Eusebius.[7] In the *Ethical Eclogues* of Stabaeus the following aphorism of Democritus is preserved,[8] which is almost exactly repeated in the fourteenth book of Eusebius,[9] namely: human beings invent for themselves the delusion of accident, a manifestation of their own perplexity, because chance (*Zufall*) battles with strong thought. Similarly Simplicius attributes to Democritus a passage in which Aristotle speaks of the old doctrine which does away with chance.[10]

By contrast Epicurus writes: "Necessity, which some make the absolute master, does not exist. There are some fortuitous things, others

[1] Id. X, 15 ... Hermippus relates that he entered a bronze bath of lukewarm water and asked for unmixed wine, which he swallowed, and then, having bidden his friends remember his doctrines, breathed his last.

[2] Cic. de Fato. X. Cic. de Nat. Deor. I, 25. Euseb. Praepar. evang. I.

[3] Aristot. de Gen. An. V, 8.

[4] Diogen. Laert. IX, 45. All things happen by virtue of necessity, the vortex being the cause of the creation of all things and this he (Democritus) calls necessity.

[5] (Plutarch.) de Placit. Philos. I.

[6] Stob. Eclog. phys. I, 2.

[7] Euseb. Praepar. evang. VI.

[8] Stob. Eclog. eth. II.

[9] Euseb. Praepar. evang. XIV.

[10] Simplic. l.c.

depend on our free will. Necessity is not to be dissuaded, but chance on the other hand is unstable. It would be better to follow the myth about the gods than to be a slave of the *heimarmenē* of the physical scientists. For the former allows the hope of mercy for honoring the gods, but the latter allows only inexorable necessity. But it is chance which it is necessary to assume, not God as the populace believes.[1] It is a misfortune to live in necessity, but it is not a necessity to live in necessity. The ways to freedom remain open everywhere, numerous, short, easy. Let us therefore thank God that no one can be held fast in life. It is permitted to subdue necessity itself." [2]

The Epicurian Velleius in Cicero says something similar about Stoic philosophy: "What are we to think of a philosophy for which, as for ignorant old women, everything seems to occur through fate? ... We have been redeemed by Epicurus, set free." [3]

Thus Epicurus even denies disjunctive judgment so as not to have to acknowledge any necessity.[4]

It is claimed that Democritus uses chance in his philosophy; but of the two passages about this which are to be found in Simplicius [5] one renders the other suspect, because it shows clearly that Democritus did not use the categories of chance, but that Simpliciers attributes them to him. He says that Democritus gives no basis for the creation of the world in general; he seems, therefore, to make chance the basis. Here we are concerned not with determining the content, but the form which Democritus consciously used. It is a similar matter with regard to the testimony of Eusebius: Democritus is said to have made chance the ruler of the universal and the divine and to have claimed that here it rules all, while keeping it separate from human life and empirical nature and calling the proclaimers of it senseless.[6]

We have, in these affirmations, the simple deductions of the Christian bishop Dionysius, that in some way where the universal and divine be-

[1] Diogen. Laert. X, 133. ... Destiny, which some introduce as sovereign over all things, he (Democritus) laughs to scorn, affirming rather that some things happen of necessity, others by chance, others through their own agency. For he sees that necessity destroys responsibility and that chance or fortune is inconstant; whereas our own actions are free, and it is to them that praise and blame naturally attach. It were better, indeed, to accept the legends of the gods than to bow beneath the yoke of destiny which the natural philosophers have imposed. The one holds out some faint hope that we may escape if we honour the gods, while the necessity of the naturalist is deaf to all entreaties.

[2] Senec. Epictol. XII.

[3] Cic. de Nat. Deor. I, 20.

[4] Ib. ib. cap. 25.

[5] Simplic. l.c. Id. l.c.

[6] Cf. Euseb. l.c. XIV.

gin the Democritean concept of necessity ceases to differ from chance.

One point then is historically certain: Democritus uses necessity, Epicurus chance. And each rejects the other's view with polemic irritability.

The most important consequence of this difference appears in the manner of explaining individual physical phenomena.

Necessity appears in finite nature, in effect, as relative necessity, as determinism. Relative necessity can only be deduced from real possibility, i.e., it is a series of conditions, causes, motives, etc., through which this necessity interposes. Real possibility is the explication of relative necessity. And this we find employed by Democritus. We shall cite as support several passages from Simplicius.

If someone is thirsty, drinks and becomes healthy, then Democritus would not give chance as the cause but rather the thirst. Because even though he seems to give chance a part in the creation of the world, nevertheless he maintains that this is not the cause in particular, and reduces it to other causes. Thus for example digging is the cause of finding treasure or vegetation the cause of the olive tree.[1]

The enthusiasm and the seriousness with which Democritus introduces this manner of explanation into his observation of nature, the importance which he attaches to the theory of the discovery of causes, are expressed with simplicity in this statement: "I would rather discover a new etiology than acquire the dignity of the Persian crown!" [2]

Once more Epicurus is directly opposed to Democritus. Chance is a reality which has only the value of possibility, abstract possibility however is precisely the antipode of real possibility. The latter is restricted by sharp boundaries, as is the understanding; the former is unbounded, like the imagination. Real possibility seeks to explain the necessity and the reality of its object; abstract possibility does not deal with the object that is explained but with the subject which explains. The object need be only possible, conceivable. What is abstractly possible, what can be conceived, constitutes for the thinking subject neither an obstacle nor a limit nor a stumbling block. Whether this possibility is also real is a matter of indifference, because we are not here interested in the object as object.

Consequently Epicurus proceeds with a boundless nonchalance in explaining individual physical phenomena.

This will become clearer from the letter to Pythocles which we shall

[1] Simplic. l.c. Cf. Id. l.c.
[2] Euseb. I.c. XIV.

have to consider later. Here let it suffice to draw attention to the opinions of earlier physical scientists. Where the author of *De placitis philosophorum* and Stobaeus quote the different views of the philosophers concerning the substance of the stars, the size and shape of the sun and similar matters, it is always said of Epicurus: He rejects no opinion, all could be right, he remains with the possible.[1] Even more, Epicurus polemicizes against the mode of explanation by real possibility which is a one-sided manner of explanation making appeal to reason.

Thus Seneca says in his *Quaestiones naturales*: Epicurus maintains that all these causes could be correct and attempts, in addition, several other explanations. He criticizes those who claim any particular one of them is correct, because it is rash to judge apodictically about that which can only be deduced from contingency.[2]

One can see that he is not at all interested in investigating the real causes of objects. He is merely interested in soothing the explaining subject. Since everything possible is admitted as possible, whatever corresponds to the character of abstract possibility is transferred from the chance of being into the chance of thinking. The unique rule which Epicurus sets forth, " the explanation may not contradict the sensible perception," is a matter of course. For abstract possibility consists precisely in the fact of being free from contradiction. This is why it is necessary to avoid contradiction.[3] Finally Epicurus admits that his manner of explanation has in view only the ataraxy of self-consciousness, not the knowledge of nature in and of itself.[4]

There is probably no need to develop this any further to show how he is in complete opposition to Democritus' position here as well.

Thus we see that both men oppose one another step by step. One is a sceptic, the other a dogmatist; one considers the sensible world subjective illusion, the other considers it objective appearance. He who considers the sensible world subjective illusion devotes himself to empirical science and to positive cognition and displays the restlessness of experimenting, universal learning, observing the wide world. The

[1] (Plutarch.) de Plac. Philosoph. II. Id. l.c. Id. ib. Stob. Eclog. phys. I.

[2] Senec. Natural. Quaest.

[3] Cf. II. Teil, 5, Kap.

Diogen. Laert. X, 88. We see how the former really takes place, but not how the celestial phenomena take place, for their occurrence may possibly be due to a variety of causes. However, we must observe each fact as presented, and further separate from it all the facts presented along with it, the occurrence of which from various causes is not contradicted by facts within our experience. ... All these alternatives are possible; they are contradicted by none of the facts in this world ...

[4] Diogen. Laert. X, 80. And we must not suppose that our treatment of these matters fails of accuracy, so far as it is needful to ensure our tranquility and happiness.

other, who considers the phenomenal world real, scorns empiricism; embodied in him are the calm of thought which finds its satisfaction in itself and the self-sufficiency that draws its knowledge *ex principio interno*. But the contrast goes even further. The sceptic and empiricist who holds nature to be subjective illusion, considers it from the point of view of necessity and endeavors to explain and to understand the real existence of things. On the other hand the philosopher and dogmatist who considers the appearance real, sees only chance everywhere, and his manner of explanation tends rather to destroy all the objective reality of nature. There seems to be a certain perversity in these contrasts.

But one can hardly expect that these men, contradicting each other in everything, will become disciples of one and the same teaching. And yet they seem to be firmly chained to one another.

To comprehend their relationship in general is the task of the next section.

PART TWO

ON THE DIFFERENCE BETWEEN THE DEMOCRITEAN AND EPICUREAN PHYSICS IN DETAIL

I. THE DECLINATION OF ATOMS FROM A STRAIGHT LINE

Epicurus assumes a threefold motion of the atoms in the void.[1] One motion is that of a fall in a straight line, the second comes from the atom deviating from a straight line, and the third is established through the repulsion of the many atoms. The assumption of the first and last motion Democritus has in common with Epicurus; the declination of the atom from the straight line differentiates them.[2]

There has been much joking about this motion of declination. Cicero more than anyone is inexhaustible when he touches on this theme. Thus we read, among other things:

Epicurus maintains that the atoms are thrust downwards by their weight in a straight line; this motion is supposed to be the natural motion of bodies. But then he notices that if all were thrust downwards, one atom would never touch another. Our man therefore takes recourse in a falsehood. He claims that the atom deviates very little – which is, of course, entirely impossible. From this arise complexities, connections and adhesions of the atoms with one another, and out of these come the world, its parts, and its contents. Besides the fact that the explanation is a puerile invention, Epicurus does not even achieve what he desires.[3]

We find another turn of phrase in the first book of the treatise "On the Nature of the Gods."

Having seen that if the atoms were driven downward by their own weight nothing would stand within our power, for their motion would be determined and neces-

[1] Stob. Eclog. phys. I. Cf. Cic. de Fin. I, 6.

[2] Cic. de Nat. Deor. I, 26.

[3] Cic .de Fin. I, 6. He (Epicurus) believes that these same indivisible solid bodies are borne by their own weight perpendicularly downward, which he holds is the natural motion of all bodies; but thereupon this clever fellow, being met with the difficulty that if they all travelled downwards in a straight line, and, as I said, perpendicularly, no one atom would ever be able to overtake any other atom, accordingly introduced an idea of his own invention: he said that the atom makes a very tiny swerve, – the smallest divergence possible; and so are produced entanglements and combinations and cohesions of atoms with atoms, which result in the creation of the world and all its parts, and of all that is in them. Now not only is the whole of this affair a piece of childish fancy, but it does not even achieve the result that its author desires.

sary, Epicurus invented a means of avoiding necessity which had escaped Democritus. He says that the atom, although thrust downward by its weight and gravity, deviates a little bit. This assertion discredits him more than if he had had to abandon his original position.[1]

A similar judgment is given by Pierre Bayle:

Before him (Epicurus), people had attributed only the motion of gravity and reflection to atoms ... Epicurus supposed that even in the middle of the void atoms deviate a little from the straight line. And from this came freedom, he said. Let us remark in passing that this was not the only motive which led him to invent this motion of deviation; he also did it to explain the coming together of atoms. For he saw clearly that in supposing that they all move downwards with an equal speed in straight lines, he would never be able to explain how they meet, and thus the creation of the world would have been impossible. It was necessary, then, that he assert that they move themselves from the straight line.[2]

For the moment I leave the validity of these reflections undiscussed. Everyone will be able to notice in passing that the most recent critic of Epicurus, Schaubach, has misunderstood Cicero when he says: "The atoms are all thrust downwards by their weight, that is, according to physical reasons, in a parallel motion. But through mutual repulsion they acquire another direction of motion, according to Cicero (*de Nat. Deor.* I, 25) an oblique motion through accidental causes and for all eternity." [3] In the first place Cicero in the quoted passage does not make repulsion the cause of oblique motion, but rather oblique motion the cause of repulsion. In the second place he does not speak of accidental causes, on the contrary he criticizes the fact that no causes at all are mentioned. Furthermore it would be contradictory for him to assert both repulsion and accidental causes as the reason for the oblique direction. At most one could then speak of accidental causes of repulsion, but not of accidental causes for the oblique direction.

In the reflections in Cicero and Bayle there is, moreover, a peculiarity too noticeable not to draw immediate attention to it. They foist upon Epicurus motives one of which denies the other. On the one hand Epicurus is supposed to have assumed the declination of atoms to explain repulsion, on the other, to explain freedom. But if the atoms do not meet apart from the motion of declination, then declination as an ex-

[1] Cic. de Nat. Deor. I, 25. Epicurus saw that if the atoms travelled downwards by their own weight, we should have no freedom of the will, since the motion of the atom would be determined by necessity. He therefore invented a device to escape from determinism (the point had apparently escaped the notice of Democritus): he said that the atom while travelling vertically downward by the force of gravity makes a very slight swerve to one side. This defence discredits him more than if he had had to abandon his original position.

[2] Bayle, Dict. hist. "Epicure."

[3] Schaubach, "Über Epikur's astronomische Begriffe" in the *Archiv für Philogie und Pädagogik* by Seebode, Jahn and Klotz, Vol. V, Fascicle IV, 1839, p. 549.

planation of freedom is superfluous; for the opposite of freedom begins as we learn from Lucretius,[1] only with the determined and forced meeting of atoms. But if the atoms meet apart from the motion of declination, then it is superfluous as an explanation of repulsion. I claim that this contradiction arises when the reasons for the declination of the atom from the straight line are taken in as superficial and illogical a way as they are by Cicero and Bayle. We find in Lucretius, the only one of all the ancients who understood the Epicurean physics, a more profound explanation.

We turn now to the consideration of the declination itself.

Just as the point is absorbed in the line, so every falling body is absorbed in the straight line which it describes. Here it is not a question of its specific quality. An apple describes a vertical line in its fall just as well as a piece of iron. Every body, in so far as it is considered in the motion of falling, is therefore nothing but a moving point, a point without autonomy, which in a certain mode of being – the straight line which it describes – renounces its individuality. Aristotle therefore correctly contends against the Pythagoreans: "You say the motion of a line is a surface, that of a point a line; then the motions of the monads will also be lines." [2] The consequence of this for monads as well as for atoms would be, since they are in constant motion,[3] that neither monad nor atom exists, but rather disappears into the straight line. For the solidity of the atom does not exist as long as it is understood as falling in a straight line. In the first place, when the void is imagined as a void in space the atom is the immediate negation of abstract space, i.e., a point in space. The solidity and intensity which maintain themselves in opposition to the incohesion of space itself, can only be added by a principle which negates space in its total sphere, such as time does in real nature. Besides, even if one did not want to admit this, the atom is, insofar as its motion is a straight line, determined purely by space, a mode of relative being is ascribed to it and its existence is purely material. But we have seen that one element in the concept of the atom is to be a pure form, the negation of all relativity, of all relation to another mode of being. We have at the same time noted that Epicurus ob-

[1] Lucret. de Rer. Nat. II, 251 sqq.

Again, if all motion is always one long chain,
and new motion always arises out of the old in order
. . . .
to infinity, whence comes this free will. . . ?

[2] Aristot. de Anima. I, 4, 14.

[1] Diogen. Laert. X, 43. Simplic. l.c.

jectifies both elements which contradict each other, but which are included in the concept of the atom.

How then can Epicurus give reality to the purely formal determination of the atom, the concept of pure individuality, which denies any mode of being determined by another thing?

Since he is working in the domain of immediate being, all determinations are immediate. Contrary determinations are therefore opposed to each other as immediate realities.

But the relative existence which is opposed to the atom, the mode of being which should negate it, is the straight line. The direct negation of this motion is another motion, thus, conceived in spatial terms, the declination from the straight line.

Atoms are purely autonomous bodies, or, rather, are bodies conceived in an absolute autonomy, like the heavenly bodies. Therefore they also move, like the latter, not in straight but in oblique lines. The motion of falling is the motion of non-autonomy.

If therefore Epicurus represents the materiality of the atom in its motion in a straight line, he has realized its formal determination in the declination from the straight line. And these opposed determinations are represented as directly opposed motions.

Lucretius therefore maintains correctly that the declination breaks through the *fati foedera*,[1] and, as he applies this directly to consciousness,[2] it can be said of the atom that declination is that in its breast which can fight back and resist.

But when Cicero reproaches Epicurus,

> for not even achieving that result in view of which he made all this up; for if all atoms decline, then none would ever combine, or some would deviate, others would be driven straight ahead by their motion. One would have to assign to the atoms as it were specific tasks according to which some would move straight ahead and some obliquely ...[3]

this objection finds its justification in that both elements included in the concept of the atom are represented as directly opposite motion. There must also be described to different particulars an inconsistency

[1] Lucret. de Rer. Nat. II, 253. sqq.

> And if the first beginnings do not make
> by swerving a beginning of motion such as to break
> the decrees of fate, that cause may not follow cause
> to infinity, whence comes this free will ...?

[2] Id. l.c. 279 sqq.

> .... an external force often propels
> men and forces them often to move on and to be hurried headlong.

[3] Cic. de Fin. I, 6.

which is consistent, however, for the sphere of the atoms is direct immediacy.

Epicurus feels in an especially strong way the contradiction which resides in this theory. He endeavors therefore to give to declination a representation as little sensible as possible. It is *nec regione loci certa nec tempore certo*;[1] (neither in a certain place nor at a fixed time) it comes into being in the smallest possible space.[2]

Cicero [3] and, according to Plutarch, several ancients, [4] make a further criticism that the declination of the atom happens without cause and no conclusion is more ignominious, says Cicero, for a physical scientist. But in the first place, a physical cause such as Cicero wants would return the declination of the atom to the sphere of determinism, which is precisely where it is supposed to emerge from.[5] But then the atom is by no means perfect in so far as it has been placed in the determination of the declination. To ask about the cause of this determination is consequently to ask about the cause which makes this atom a principle element – a question which is clearly senseless in the eyes of those for whom the atom is the cause of everything but is itself without cause.

Finally Bayle,[6] supported by the authority of Augustine,[7] (according to whom Democritus ascribed to the atoms a spiritual principle – an authority, which by the way, in view of the contrast with Aristotle and the other ancients, is completely unimportant), reproaches Epicurus for having conceived of declination instead of this spiritual principle. The concept of the declination, contrary to this opinion, to speak of the soul of the atom, would merely add a word. While in declination the real soul of the atom, the concept of abstract individuality, is represented.

Before we consider the consequence of the declination of the atom from the straight line, there is still a highly important element to be stressed which has been totally overlooked until now.

The declination of the atom from the straight line is in fact not a particular determination appearing accidentally in the Epicurean physics. The law which it expresses runs through the whole Epicurean philosophy. But it does so in such a way, naturally, that the fixed form of its appearance is dependent upon the sphere in which it is applied.

[1] Lucret. l.c. II, 293 sqq.
[2] Cic. de Fato. X.
[3] Id ib.
[4] Plutarch. de Anim. procreat. VI.
[5] Cic. de Fin. I, 6.
[6] Bayle l.c.
[7] August. Epist. 56.

As a matter of fact, the abstract individuality can affirm its concept, its determination of form, its pure being-for-itself, its independence from every direct mode of being, its suppression of all relativity, only by making an abstraction of the being that comes into opposition to it. For in order to overcome it truly, it must idealize it, which only generality can do.

Thus as the atom frees itself from its relative existence, the straight line, by making an abstraction of it, by evading it, so the whole Epicurean philosophy evades the restrictive mode of being whenever the concept of abstract individuality, the autonomy and negation of all relation to other things, might be represented in its existence.

Thus the goal of action is abstraction, the avoidance of pain and confusion, *ataraxy*.[1] Thus the good consists in avoiding the bad [2] and happiness is avoidance of pain.[3] Finally, where abstract individuality appears at het highest point of its freedom and autonomy, in its totality, then logically the mode of being is evaded in all existence; and thus the gods evade the world and do not concern themselves with it and dwell outside it.[4]

People have poked fun at these gods of Epicurus who, similar to men, live in the inner regions of the real world. They have no body but a quasi-body, no blood but quasi-blood,[5] and subsisting in blissful peace, hear no supplication. They are unconcerned about men and the world, honored because of their beauty, their majesty and their superior nature, not for any gain.

And yet these gods are not a fiction of Epicurus. They do exist. They are the plastic gods of Greek art. Cicero rails at them with reason[6]; but Plutarch the Greek forgot every Greek concept when he opines that this theory of the gods gives evidence to fear and superstition, that it attributes to the gods no joy nor favor, but rather it gives man the relationship to gods that we have to the Hyranian fish, from which we expect neither harm nor advantage.[7] Theoretical calm is a chief element in the character of Greek divinities. As Aristotle says: "What is best requires no action, for it itself is its own end." [8]

We consider now the consequence that directly arises out of the de-

[1] Diogen. Laert. X, 128.
[2] Plutarch. de eo, quod sec. Epicur. non beate vivi poss.
[3] Clem. Alex. Strom. II.
[4] Senec. de Benef. IV.
[5] Cic. de Nat. Deor. I, 24.
[6] Cic. de Nat. Deor. I, 38, 39.
[7] Plutarch. de eo, quod sec. Epicur, non beate vivi poss.
[8] Aristot. de Caelo. II, 12.

clination of the atom. What is expressed here is that the atom negates all motion and relation wherein it is determined by another as a particular being. This is represented in that the atom makes an abstraction of the mode of being that opposes it, and withdraws itself from this opposing element. But that which is here contained, its negation of all relation to something else, must be made real, positively established. This can only be done if the being to which it refers is none other than itself, thus equally an atom, and, since it itself is directly determined, many atoms. Thus the repulsion of the many atoms is a necessary realization of the *lex atomi*, as Lucretius calls the declination. But because here every determination is established as a particular being, so repulsion is added as a third motion to the earlier ones. Lucretius says correctly that if the atoms were not accustomed to decline, neither repulsion nor encounter would have arisen, and the world would never have been created.[1] For atoms are their own unique object and have reference only to themselves. Consequently, expressed in terms of space, they meet one another only when every relative aspect of their being, in which they are related to something else, is negated. This relative existence is, as we have seen, their original motion, that of falling in a straight line. Thus they meet only through their declination. It is not a matter of purely material scattering.[2]

In truth, the immediately existing individual is realized according to its concept only insofar as it refers to an other which is itself, even if the other thing appears as its opposite in the form of immediate existence. Thus it is that man ceases to be a product of nature only if the

[1] Lucret. de Rer. Nat. II, 221 sqq.

> .... they swerve a little from their
> course, just so much as you might call a change of
> motion. For if they were not apt to incline, all
> would fall downwards like raindrops through the
> profound void, no collision would take place and no
> blow would be caused amongst the first beginnings:
> thus nature would never have produced anything.

[2] Lucret. de Rer. Nat. II, 284 sqq.

> .... Wherefore you must
> admit that the same exists in the seeds also, that
> motions have some cause other than blows and
> weights, from which this power is born in us, since
> we see that nothing can be produced from nothing.
>
> . . . .
>
> .... For it is weight that prevents all things from
> being caused through blows by a sort of external force;
> but what keeps the mind itself from having necessity
> within it in all actions and from being as it were
> mastered and forced to endure and to suffer this, is
> the minute swerving of the first-beginnings at no fixed
> place and at no fixed time.

other thing, to which he is related, is not a different existence but rather itself an individual human being, furthermore not the spirit. But in order for man to become his only true object, he must have crushed within himself his relative mode of being, the force of passion and of mere nature. Repulsion is the first form of self-consciousness; it corresponds therefore to the self-consciousness which comprehends itself as an immediately existing entity, an abstractly individual thing.

Hence in repulsion the concept of the atom is realized according to which it is abstract form, but the contrary is also realized according to which it is abstract matter; for that to which it refers is indeed atoms, but other atoms. Now, if I relate to myself as to something directly other, then my relating is a material one. This is the highest degree of externality that can be conceived. In the repulsion of the atoms, therefore, their materiality which was established as the downward fall in a straight line and their formal determination which was established in declination, these are synthetically united.

Democritus, in contrast to Epicurus, transforms an act of blind necessity into a powerful motion, that which for Epicurus is a realization of the concept of the atom. We have already seen that he gives substance to the vortex (*dinē*) which results from the repulsion and collision of atoms. He therefore envisions in repulsion only the material side, the scattering, the change, not the ideal side, according to which all relation to something other is negated and motion is established as self-determination. This we can clearly see from the fact that Democritus conceives of one and the same body sensibly divided by empty space into many parts, like gold that is broken into many pieces.[1] Thus he scarcely conceives the One as the concept of the atom.

Aristotle correctly argues against him:

Leucippus and Democritus, who assert that primary bodies always move in the void and the infinite, should indicate what sort of motion this is, and what is the motion adequate to their nature. In effect, if each of the elements is put into motion by another by force, still it is necessary that each also have a natural motion, besides that which is by force. And this first motion must not be one of force, but natural. Otherwise the progression extends to infinity.[2]

[1] Aristot. de Caelo. I, 7. If the whole is not continuous, but its elements are separated by the void (as in the theory of Democritus and Leucippus), then the motion of all will of necessity be one .... The nature of all atoms is, they say, the same, just as if, e.g. each one separately were a piece of gold.

[2] Aristot. de Caelo. III, 2. When therefore Leucippus and Democritus speak of the primary bodies as always moving in the infinite void, they ought to say with what motion they move and what is their natural motion. Each of the atoms may be forcibly moved by another, but each one must have some natural motion also, from which the enforced motion diverges. Moreover the original motion cannot act by force, but only naturally. We shall go on to

The Epicurean declination of the atom thus changed the whole inner construction of the realm of the atoms, by making valid the determination of form through it and by realizing the contradiction which lies in the concept of the atom. Consequently, Epicurus was the first, even if only in sensible form, to have grasped the essence of repulsion, while Democritus only understood its material existence.

Therefore we also find more concrete forms of repulsion applied by Epicurus; in the political sphere it is the contract,[1] in the social sphere friendship[2] which is praised as the highest.

II. The Qualities of the Atom

It is contradictory to the concept of the atom to have qualities, because, as Epicurus says, every quality is changeable, but the atoms do not change.[3] But it is nevertheless a necessary consequence of attributing qualities to atoms. For the plurality of atoms in repulsion, separated by sensible space, must necessarily be directly opposite each other and different from their pure being, i.e. must possess qualities.

Consequently in the following discussion I take no account at all of Schneider's and Nurnberger's claim that Epicurus ascribed no qualities to the atoms, and that paragraphs 44 and 54 in the letter to Herodotus in Diogenes Laertius are forged. If this were really so, how is one to invalidate all the testimony of Lucretius, of Plutarch, indeed of all writers who speak of Epicurus? Moreover, Diogenes Laertius mentions the qualities of the atoms not in two, but in ten paragraphs: 42, 43, 44, 54, 55, 56, 57, 58, 59 and 61. The reason which these critics give, that "they have no idea how to unite the qualities of the atom with its concept," is very insipid. Spinoza says that ignorance is no argument. If everyone wanted to strike out the passages in the ancients which he did not understand, how quickly would we have *tabula rasa*!

Through the qualities the atom acquires an existence which contra-

infinity if there is to be no first thing which imparts motion naturally, but always a prior one which moves because itself set in motion by force.

[1] Diogen. Laert. X, 150. Those animals which are incapable of making covenants with one another, to the end that they may neither inflict nor suffer harm, are without either justice or injustice. And those tribes which either could not or would not form mutual covenants to the same end are in like case.

[2] Id.

[3] Diogen. Laert. X, 54. For every quality changes, but the atoms do not change.

Lucret. de Rer. Nat. II, 861 sqq.

> All these things must be kept apart from the
> first-beginnings, if we wish to lay an
> imperishable foundation for things upon
> which the sum of existence may rest.

dicts its concept, it is presented in a mode of alienated being differentiated from its essence. It is this contradiction which constitutes the main interest of Epicurus. Therefore, as soon as he poses a quality and thus has drawn out the result of the material nature of the atom, he counterposes at the same time determinations which again destroy this quality in its own sphere and, on the contrary, make the concept of the atom valid. He determines, therefore, all qualities in such a way that they contradict themselves. Democritus on the other hand nowhere considers the qualities in relation to the atom itself, nor does he objectify the internal contradiction between concept and existence. Rather his whole interest lies in representing the qualities in relation to concrete nature which is to be formed out of them. To him they are merely hypotheses to explain the multiplicity which appears. The concept of the atom has therefore nothing to do with them.

In order to demonstrate our claim, it is first of all necessary to come to terms with the sources which seem to contradict each other on the point we have just mentioned.

In the treatise *De placitis philosophorum* we read: "Epicurus claims that these three things are to be ascribed to the atoms: size, form, weight. Democritus only assumed two: size and form; Epicurus added to these, weight as a third." [1] The same passage is found repeated verbatim in the *Praeparatio evangelica* of Eusebius. [2]

It is confirmed by the testimony of Simplicius [3] and Philoponus,[4] according to whom Democritus attributed to the atoms only the difference of size and form. Directly contrary is the testimony of Aristotle, who, in the first book of *De generatione et corruptione,* ascribes different weight to Democritus' atoms.[5] In another passage (in the first book of *De caelo*) Aristotle leaves undecided the question as to whether or not Democritus ascribed weight to the atoms. He says: "Thus none of the bodies will be absolutely light if they all have weight; but if all have lightness, none will be heavy." [6] Ritter in his *Geschichte der alten Philosophie* rejects the assertions of Plutarch, Eusebius and Stobaeus, sup-

[1] (Plutarch.) de Plac. Philosoph. I, 28 sqq.
Cf. Sext. Empir. adv. Math. p. 421.
[2] Euseb. Praepar. evang. XIV.
[3] Simplic. l.c.
[4] Philopon. ibid.
[5] Aristot. de Gen. et Corrupt. I, 8.
[6] Aristot. de Caelo. I, 7. All atoms must, as we have just said, have the same motion. ... Therefore none of the atoms will be absolutely light, if they all have weight, nor heavy if all have lightness. Again, if they have either weight or lightness, the universe will have either a farthest limit or a centre.

porting himself with the authority of Aristotle[1]; he does not take into consideration the testimony of Simplicius and Philoponus.

Let us see if these passages are really so contradictory. In the cited passages Aristotle speaks of the qualities of the atom not *ex professo*. On the other hand we read in the seventh book of the *Metaphysics*: "Democritus establishes three distinctions among atoms. For the fundamental body is, with respect to matter, one and the same; it differs however in (*rhusmos*), which means form, in (*trope*), which means situation, and in (*diathige*), meaning order." [2] Much can be concluded from this passage immediately: weight is not mentioned as a quality of the Democritean atoms. The scattered particulars of matter, kept apart by the void, must have particular forms, adopted quite externally in regard to the void. This idea comes out even more clearly in the following passage of Aristotle: "Leucippus and his companion Democritus say that the elements are the plenum and the void..... These are the basis of material being. Just as those who assert that a unique, fundamental substance gives rise to all else by their affections, assuming as principles the qualities of rarefaction and density; in the same way the above-mentioned also teach that the distinctions between atoms are the causes of all else for the being lying at the basis differentiates itself only in *rhusmos*, *diathige* and *trope* ... That is, A differs from N in form, An from Na in order, Z from N in situation." [3]

It is evidently to be concluded from this passage that Democritus considers the qualities of the atoms only in connection with the formation of distinctions in the world of appearance, not in connection with the atom itself. It follows further that Democritus does not emphasize weight as an essential quality of the atoms. It is self-evident to him because everything corporeal is heavy. Equally, according to him size is not a basic quality. It is an accidental determination which is already given to the atoms with form. Only the difference between the

[1] Ritter. Geschichte d. alt. Philosophie. Part I.

[2] Aristot. Metaphys. VII (VIII), 2.

[3] Aristot. Metaphys. I, 4. Leucippus, however, and his disciple Democritus hold that the elements are the Full and the Void – calling the one "what is" and the other "what is not." Of these they identify the full or solid with "what is," and the void or rare with "what is not" (hence they hold that what is not is no less real than what is, because Void is as real as Body); and they say that these are the material causes of things. And just as those who make the underlying substance a unity generate all other things by means of its modifications, assuming rarity and density as first principles of these modifications, so these thinkers hold that the "differences" are the causes of everything else. These differences, they say, are three: shape, arrangement, and position; because they hold that what is differs only in *contour*, *inter-contact*, and *inclination*, (of these contour means shape, inter-contact arrangement, and inclination position.) Thus, e.g. A differs from N in shape, AN from NA in arrangement, and Z from N in position.

configurations – because nothing further is contained in form, situation, position – interests Democritus. Size, form, weight, by being put together as is done by Epicurus, are differences which the atom itself has; form, situation, order, are differences which are ascribed to it in respect to another object. While we find in Democritus mere hypothetical determinations for the explanation of the phenomenal world, in Epicurus the consequence of the principle itself is presented to us. We shall therefore consider his determinations of the qualities of the atom in detail.

In the first place the atoms have size.[1] On the other hand size is also negated. They do not have every size,[2] but there are only some differences of size among them to be posited.[3] Indeed only the negation of size is to be ascribed to them, that is, smallness,[4] not the minimum size, because this would be a purely spatial determination, but it is an infinite smallness which expresses the contradiction.[5] Rosinius in his notes to the *Fragments* of Epicurus translates one passage incorrectly and overlooks the other completely when he says:

> huius modi autem tenuitatem atomorum incredibili parvitate arguebat Epicurus, utpote quas nulla magnitudine praeditas aiebat teste Laertio X, 44 [6]

We will pay no heed to that assertion of Eusebius that Epicurus was the first to ascribe infinite smallness to the atoms,[7] for Democritus also posited (Stobaeus even affirms this [8]) atoms of the largest size – large as the world.

On the one hand the testimony of Aristotle [9] contradicts this. On the other hand, Eusebius, or rather the Alexandrian bishop Dionysius, from whom he takes excerpts, contradicts himself. For in the same book we read that Democritus asserts the primary elements of nature to be

[1] Diogen. Laert. X, 44. He says below that atoms have no qualities at all except shape, size, and weight ... that they are not of any and every size; at any rate no atom has ever been seen by our senses.

[2] Id. X, 56. But to attribute any and every magnitude to the atoms does not help to explain the difference of quality in things; moreover, in that case atoms large enough to be seen ought to have reached us, which is never observed to occur; nor can we conceive how its occurrence should be possible, i.e. that an atom should become visible.

[3] Id. X, 55. Again, you should not suppose that the atoms have any and every size ... but difference of size must be admitted.

[4] Id. X, 59. It is only in minuteness that the atom differs from that which is observed by sense.

[5] Cf. Id. X, 58. Stob. Eclog. phys. I.

[6] Epicuri fragm. (de Nat. II et XI).

[7] Euseb. Praepar. evang. XIV.

[8] Stob. Eclog. phys. I, 17. Cf. (Plutarch.) de Placit. Philosoph. I.

[9] Aristot. de Gener. et Corrupt. I, 8.

indivisible bodies perceptible through reason.[1] But this much is clear, Democritus does not give conscious attention to the contradiction; it does not occupy him, while it forms Epicurus' chief interest.

The second quality of the Epicurean atoms is form.[2] But this determination also contradicts the concept of the atom, and its opposite must be posited. Abstract individuality is abstract identity with itself and therefore without form. The differences in form among atoms are, it is true, indeterminate,[3] but they are not absolutely infinite.[4] Rather it is a determined and finite number of forms by which the atoms are differentiated.[5] From this it is self-evident that there are not as many different forms as there are atoms,[6] while Democritus posits an infinite number of forms.[7] If each atom had a particular form, then there would have to be atoms of infinite size,[8] because they would have an infinite difference, a differentation from all the others, like the monads of Leibniz. The statement of Leibniz, that no two things are the same, is therefore turned about, and there are infinitely many atoms of the same form.[9]

[1] Euseb. Praepar. evang. XIV.

[2] Diogen. Laert. X, 54. Moreover, we must hold that the atoms in fact possess none of the qualities belonging to things which come under our observation, except shape, weight, and size, and the properties necessarily conjoined with shape.

[3] Id. X, 42.

[4] Id. Ib.

[5] Lucret. II, 513 sqq. It must be confessed that matter also has a limited number of different shapes.

Euseb. Praepar. evang. XIV.

[6] Diogen. Laert. X, 42.

Lucret. II, 525 sqq. Indeed since the difference of shapes is finite, it is necessary that the shapes which are alike be infinite, or else that the sum of matter be finite, which I have proved not to be so.

[7] Aristot. de Caelo. III, 4. There is another view, championed by Leucippus and Democritus of Abdera, whose conclusions are no more acceptable to reason, ... If shape is the distinguishing feature of bodies, and there is an infinite number or shapes, they are asserting an infinite number of simple bodies. Yet they never went so far as to define or characterize the shape of each element, except to assign the sphere to fire.

Philopon. l.c.

[8] Lucret. de Rer. Nat. l.c. II, 479 sqq.

> .... The first-beginnings have
> a finite number of different shapes. If
> that were not so, it would once more fol-
> low that some of the seeds will necessarily
> be of infinite size. For within the same small
> measure of one given body the shapes can-
> not differ much from one another ...
> .... if after
> all you wish perhaps to vary the shapes,
> other parts must be added ....
> Therefore novelty of shapes implies in-
> crease of size. Wherefore it is impossible
> for you to believe that the seeds have an
> infinite number of differing shapes.

[9] Cf. Not. 25

This scheme clearly indicates that the determination of form is negated again, because a form which does not differentiate itself from others is not a form.

Finally it is highly important that Epicurus introduced weight as a third quality,[1] because in the point of gravity matter possesses ideal particularity which constitutes a primary determination of the atom. Once the atoms are brought into the realm of representations then they must be heavy.

But weight also directly contradicts the concept of the atom, because it is the particularity of matter as an ideal point which lies outside of it. But the atom is itself this particularity, as it were the center of gravity, imagined as an individual existence. Therefore weight exists for Epicurus only as differing weight, and the atoms are themselves substantial centers of gravity, like the heavenly bodies. If one applies this to the concrete world, then the fact becomes self-evident which old Brucker finds so amazing [2] and of which Lucretius assures us,[3] namely, that the earth has no center toward which everything tends and that there are no antipodes. Furthermore, since weight is only ascribed to atoms differentiated from others, i.e. ones endowed with qualities, then it is clear that where the atoms are thought of not as a plurality in their differentiation from each other, but only in connection with the void, the determination of weight vanishes. The atoms, as different as they may be in mass and form, move therefore with equal speed in empty space.[4] Epicurus therefore applies weight only in regard to repulsion and combinations which arise from repulsion, which has given rise to

[1] Diogen. Laert. X, 44 et 54.

[2] Bruckeri Instit, histor. phil. p. 24.

[3] Lucret. de Rer. Nat. I, 1051

> One belief concerning these matters, Memmius, you must avoid and keep afar: that as some say, all things press toward the centre of the whole.

[4] Diogen. Laert. X, 43. The atoms move with equal speed, since the void makes way for the lightest and heaviest alike. When they are travelling through the void and meet with no resistance, the atoms must move with equal speed. Neither will heavy atoms travel more quickly than small and light ones, so long as nothing meets them, nor will small atoms travel more quickly than large ones, provided they always find a passage suitable to their size, and provided also that they meet with no obstruction.

Lucret. de Rer. Nat. II, 235 sqq.

> But contrariwise empty void cannot offer any support to anything anywhere or at any time, but it must give way continually as its nature demands: wherefore they must all be carried with equal speed, although not of equal weight, through the unresisting void.

the claim that only conglomerations of atoms, but not atoms themselves, are endowed with weight.[1]

Gassendi praises Epicurus that he, led purely by reason, anticipated the experienced fact whereby all bodies highly different in weight and mass fall downward with equal speed.[2]

The consideration of the qualities of the atoms provides us therefore with the same result as the consideration of declination, namely that Epicurus objectifies the contradiction in the concept of the atom between essence and existence and thus provides science with the theory of the atoms, while in Democritus no realization of the principle element itself takes place, but only the material side is maintained and hypotheses offered in support of empirical investigation.

III. *ATOMOI ARCHAI* AND *ATOMA STOICHEIA*

Chaubach, in the treatise already cited above on the astronomical concepts of Epicurus, affirms:

> Epicurus, as well as Aristotle, made a distinction between atoms without origin (*atomoi archai*, Diogen. Laert. X, 41) and elementary atoms (*atoma stoicheia*, Diogen. Laert. X, 86). The former are the atoms knowable only through the intellect, they fill no space ...[3]

They are called atoms, not because they are the smallest bodies, but because they are not divisible in space. According to these ideas one is supposed to believe that Epicurus ascribed no spatial qualities to the atoms.[4] But in the letter to Herodotus (Diogen. Laert. X, 44, 54) he gives the atoms not only weight, but also form and size.... "I therefore arrange these atoms in the second category, those which have arisen out of the former but are still regarded as elementary parts of bodies." [5]

Let us look more closely at the passage which Schaubach cites from Diogenes Laertius. It reads: *hoion hoti to pan sōma kai anaphēs phusis estin ē hoti atoma stocheia kai panta ta toiauta.*[6]

[1] Vg. Kap. 3.

[2] Feuerbachs Geschichte d. neueren Philosophie. 1833. XXXIII, 7.

[3] *Ametocha kenou* does not mean "fill no space," but "do not partake of the void," it is the same as when it is said elsewhere in Diogenes Laertius "*dialeipsin de merōn ouk echousin.*" This expression is to be explained similarly in (Plutarch) de Placit. Philosoph. I, p. 286 and Simplicius p. 405.

[4] This too is a false conclusion. What cannot be divided in space is not for that reason outside space and without spatial connection.

[5] Schaubach l.c. p. 550.

[6] Diogen. Laert. X, 44.

Epicurus here informs Pythocles, to whom he is writing, that the doctrine of the meteors differs from all other physical doctrines. For example, that everything is body and void, that there are indivisible basic materials. One can see that there is no reason here to assume that he is talking about a secondary category of atoms. Perhaps it seems that the distinction between *to pan sōma kai anaphēs physis* and *hoti ta atoma stoicheia* posits a difference between *sōma* and *atoma stoicheia,* whereby we might say that *sōma* means the atoms of the first kind in contrast to the *atoma stoicheia.* But this is quite out of the question. *Sōma* means the corporeal in contrast to the void, which therefore also is called *asōmation.*[1] *Sōma,* therefore designates atoms as well as compounded bodies. So it is said for example in the letter to Herodotus: *to pan esti sōma . . . ei mē ēn ho kenon kai chōran kai anaphē phusin onomadzomen . . . tōn sōmatōn ta aen esti sugkriseis, ta d ex hōn hai sugkriseis pepoiēntai tauta me estin atoma kai ametablēta . . . hōste tas archas atomous dnagkaion einai sōmatōn phuseis.*[2] In the passage cited above Epicurus first speaks of the corporeal in general in contrast to the void, then of the corporeal in particular, the atoms.

Schaubach's appeal to Aristotle proves just as little. The difference between *archē* and *stocheion,* which is primarily urged by the Stoics,[3] is also to be found in Aristotle,[4] but nonetheless he asserts the identity of both expressions.[5] He even expressly teaches that *stoicheion* denotes primarily the atom.[6] Equally Leucippus and Democritus also call the *plēres kai kenon "stoicheion."* [7]

In Lucretius, in the letters of Epicurus in Diogenes Laertius, in the Colotes of Plutarch,[8] in Sextus Empiricus,[9] qualities are ascribed to atoms themselves, whereby they are represented as annulling themselves.

If it is to be regarded as an antimony, however, that perceptible bodies are endowed with spatial qualities merely through reason, then it is a much greater antinomy that the spatial qualities themselves can only be perceived through the intellect.[10]

1 Id. X, 67.
2 Id. X, 39, 40 and 41.
3 Id. VII, 1.
4 Aristot. Metaphys. IV, 1 and 3.
5 Cf. l.c.
6 Aristot. l.c. 3.
7 Aristot. Metaphys. I, 4.
8 Diogen. Laert. X, 54. (Plutarch.) Colot.
9 Sext. Emp. adv. Match.
10 Euseb. Praepar. evang. XIV.

Finally, Schaubach quotes as a further proof of his view the following passage from Stobaeus: *Epikouros ... ta próta* (sc. *sōmata*) *men hapla, ta d ex ekeinōn sugkrimata panta Baros echein.* To this passage in Stobaeus the following could also be added in which *atoma stoicheia* are mentioned as a particular kind of atom: (Plutarch, *De placitis philosophorum*, I, 26 and 249, and Stob. *Eclog. phys.* I, p. 5).[1] Incidentally, it is by no means claimed in these passages that the aboriginal atoms are without size, form and weight. Rather, weight is only spoken of as a differentiating characteristic of *atomoi archai* and *atoma stoicheia.* But we noted already in the preceding chapter that weight is only applied in regard to repulsion and the conglomerations arising out of it.

With the invention of *atoma stoicheia* nothing is gained. It is as difficult to pass from the *atomoi archai* to the *atoma stoicheia* as to ascribe qualities to them directly. Nevertheless I do not deny this distinction entirely. The only thing I deny is that there are two fixed and different species of atoms. These are, on the contrary, different determinations of one and the same species.

Before examining this difference, I call attention to Epicurus' procedure. Namely, he likes to posit the diverse determination of a concept as different, autonomous existences. Just as his principle is the atom, so the manner of his knowledge itself is atomistic. Without his suspecting it, every element of development transforms itself immediately into a fixed reality as it were separated from its context by empty space; all determination takes on the form of isolated particularity.

This manner will become clear from the following example:

The infinite, *to apeiron,* or the *infinitio,* as Cicera translates it, is used from time to time as a particular nature by Epicurus; indeed in the same passages in which we find the *stoicheia* determined as a fixed, basic substance, so we also find the *apeiron* rendered independent.[2]

But according to Epicurus' own determinations the infinite is neither a particular substance nor something outside of the atoms and the void, but rather an accidental determination of them. We find in fact three meanings for *apeiron.*

First *apeiron* expresses for Epicurus a quality which is common to atoms and the void. Thus it means the infinitude of the universe which is infinite by virtue of the infinite multiciplity of the atoms, by virtue of the infinite size of the void.[3]

[1] (Plutarch.) de Placit. Philosoph. I. (VII, 1074).
Stob. Eclog phys. I.

[2] Cf. l.c. Cic. de Fin. I, 6. Diogen. Laert. X, 41.

[3] (17) omitted).

Another time *apeiria* is the multiplicity of the atoms, so that not the atom, but the infinitely many atoms are opposed to the void.[1]

Finally, if we can draw a conclusion from Democritus which will be valid for Epicurus, *apeiron* means also just the opposite, the unbounded void, which is opposed to the determined atom bounded by itself.[2]

In all these meanings – and they are the only ones, even the only possible ones for the atomic theory – the infinite is a mere determination of the atoms and the void. Nevertheless, it is rendered independent as a particular existence, even set up as a specific nature next to the primary elements whose determination it expresses.

Therefore let Epicurus himself have made the determination by which the atom becomes *stoicheion* as an autonomous, primary species of atoms; (which, by the way, drawing a conclusion from the historical superiority of one source over the other, is not the case), or let Metrodorus, the pupil of Epicurus, which seems improbable to us, be the first to have transformed diverse determination into differing existence[3]: we must blame the subjective mode of the atomistic consciousness for rendering individual elements independent. By providing the diverse determinations with the form of differing existence, people have not comprehended their difference.

The atom has for Democritus only the meaning of a *stoicheion*, of substrative matter. The distinction between the atom as *archē* and *stoicheion*, as principle element and basis, belongs to Epicurus. Its importance will become clear from the following.

The contradiction between existence and essence, between matter and form which lies in the concept of the atom, is attributed to the individual atom by endowing it with qualities. Through its quality the atom is alienated from its concept, but at the same time perfected in its construction. Out of repulsion and the conglomerations of the qualitied atoms arises now the world of appearance.

In this passage from the world of essence into the world of appearance the contradiction in the concept of the atom clearly reaches its most vivid realization. For according to its concept, the atom is the absolute, essential form of nature. This absolute form is now degraded to absolute matter, to a formless substratum of the world of appearance.

1 Plutarch. Colot. XIII.
2 Simplic. l.c.
3 (Plutarch.) de Placit. Philoso. I, V.

Atoms are, to be sure, the substance of nature [1] out of which everything arises, into which everything dissolves[2]; but the constant annihilation of the world of appearance comes to no result. New appearances are formed; the atom itself remains always at the bottom as sediment. Thus insofar as the atom is thought of according to its pure concept, empty space, annihilated nature is its existence; insofar as it comes into reality it sinks down to a material basis which, as the bearer of a world of multitudinous relations, never exists except in its indifferent and external form.[3] This is a necessary consequence because the atom, conceived as an absrtact and complete particular, cannot affirm itself as an idealizing and dominating power over that multiplicity.

Abstract particularity is freedom from being, not freedom in being. It cannot shine in the light of being. There it is an element whereby it loses its character and becomes material. Therefore, the atom does not manifest itself in the light of appearance,[4] or it sinks down to a material basis when it does enter it. The atom as such exists only in the void. Thus the death of nature has become its immortal substance, and Lucretius correctly asserts:

mortalem vitam mors quum immortalis ademit

But the fact that Epicurus grasps this contradiction at this its highest point and objectifies it, (i.e. distinguishes the atom where it

[1] Lucret. de Rer. Nat. I, 820 sqq.

For the same beginnings constitute sky, sea, earth,
rivers, sun, the same make crops, trees, animals.

Diogen. Laert. X, 39. And if that which disappears had been destroyed and become non-existent, everything would have perished, that into which the things were dissolved being non-existent. ... The whole of being consists of bodies and space. ... These elements are indivisible and unchangeable, and necessarily so, if things are not all to be destroyed and pass into non-existence, but are to be strong enough to endure when the composite bodies are broken up, because they possess a solid nature and are incapable of being anywhere or anyhow dissolved.

[2] Diogen. Laert. X, 73. For all these, whether small or great, have been separated from special conglomerations of atoms, and all things are again dissolved, some faster, some slower, some through the action of one set of causes, others through the action of another.

Lucret. V, 108 sqq.

And may pure reason rather than experience
persuade, that the universe can collapse
borne down with a frightful-sounding crash.

Id. V, 374

The door of death therefore is not closed for
the heavens, not for the sun and earth and the
deep waters of the sea, but stands open and
awaits them with vast and hideous arms.

[3] Simplic. l.c.

[4] Lucret. II, 796

The first-beginnings of things do not
come out into the light.

becomes a basis of appearance as *stoicheion* from the atom as it exists in the void as *archē*), is what constitutes his philosophical difference from Democritus, who only objectifies the one element. It is the same difference which separated Epicurus and Democritus in the world of essence, the realm of the atoms and the void. But since only the qualitied atom is the perfected one, since the world of appearance can only proceed out of the perfected atom which has been alienated from its concept, so Epicurus expresses this by saying that only the qualitied atom becomes *stoicheion* or that the *atomon stoicheion* is endowed with qualities.

IV. Time

Since in the atom, matter, as pure relationship to itself, is removed from all mutability and relativity, it immediately follows that time is to be excluded from the concept of the atom, from the world of essence. For matter is only eternal and autonomous insofar as one makes an abstraction of the temporal element within it. Here Democritus and Epicurus agree. But they differ in the manner in which time, removed from the world of atoms, is determined, whither it is transferred.

For Democritus time has neither importance nor necessity for the system. He explains it in order to dispose of it. It is determined as eternal so that, as Aristotle [1] and Simplicius [2] say, birth and death, i.e. the temporal, are removed from the atoms. Time itself offers proof that not everything need have an origin, a movement of beginning.

There is a more profound matter to be recognized here. The imagining intellect, which does not comprehend the autonomy of substance, asks about its temporal becoming. The point escapes him that by making substance into something temporal, he at the same time makes time into something substantial and therewith destroys its concept, because time made absolute is no longer temporal.

But from another point of view this solution is unsatisfying. Time, excluded from the world of essence, is transferred to the self-consciousness of the philosophizing subject, but does not make contact with the world itself.

Epicurus treats it differently. Excluded from the world of essence, time for him becomes the absolute form of appearance. Indeed it is

[1] Aristot. Phys. VIII, 1. It is thus that Democritus shows how impossible it is that everything can have had an origin – because time has not.

[2] Simplic. l.c.

determined as accidents of accidents. Accident is the change of substance in general. The accident of accident is the change as reflected within itself, change as change. This pure form of the world of appearance is thus time.[1]

Combination is the merely passive form of concrete nature, time its active form. If I consider combination according to its being, then the atom exists beyond it in the void, in imagination. If I consider the atom according to its concept, then combination either does not exist at all or only in the subjective idea. For combination is a connection in which the autonomous atoms, confined to themselves, as it were disinterested in one another, are equally unrelated to one another. On the other hand, time, the change of the finite, by being posited as change, is also the real form which separates the appearance from the essence, posits it as appearance, as it leads back into essence. Combination expresses the materiality of the atoms as well as of nature that rises out of them. Time on the other hand is to the world of appearance what the concept of the atom is to the world of essence, namely the abstraction, annihilation and reduction of all determined being into being-for-itself.

From this consideration the following conclusions are to be drawn. First, Epicurus makes the contradiction between matter and form the character of phenomenal nature, which thus becomes the opposite of essential nature, the atom. This happens in that time is opposed to space, the active form of appearance is opposed to the passive. Second, only in Epicurus is appearance comprehended as appearance, that is as an alienation of the essence which asserts itself as alienation in its reality. On the other hand, in Democritus, for whom combination is the only form of phenomenal nature, appearance does not exhibit itself as appearance, something different from essence. If we consider appearance as to its existence, essence is totally confused with it; if we consider appearance as to its concept it is entirely separated from it. Appearance is thus degraded to the state of subjective illusion. Combination

[1] Lucret. I, 459 sqq.

> Time also exists not of itself . . . .
> . . . .
> Nor may we admit that anyone has a sense
> of time by itself separated from the movement
> of things and quiet calm.

Id. I, 479 sqq.

> Things do never at all consist or exist in
> themselves as body does, nor are said to
> exist in the same way as void; but rather
> you may properly call them accidents of body.

Sext. Empir. adv. Math. Stob. Eclog. Phys. I, 9.

behaves indifferently and materially as opposed to its essential bases. Time, on the other hand, is the fire of essence which eternally consumes appearance and stamps it with the character of dependence and non-being. Finally, time, being, according to Epicurus, change as change, reflection of appearance in itself, phenomenal nature is correctly posited as objective, sensible perception, is correctly made the real criterion of concrete nature, although the atom, its basis, is only grasped through reason.

Indeed, time being the abstract form of sensible perception, the necessity exists, in conformity with the atomistic manner of the Epicurean consciousness, that it be determined within nature as a particular existence. The mutability of the sensible world as mutability, its change as change, this reflection of appearance in itself which forms the concept of time, has its particular existence in conscious sensibility. The sensibility of man is therefore embodied time, the existing reflection of the world of sense in itself.

As this can be concluded immediately from the determination of the concept of time in Epicurus, so it can be quite definitely demonstrated in detail. In Epicurus' letter to Herodotus [1] time is so represented that it arises when the accidents of the body perceived by the senses are thought of as accidents. Sense perception reflected in itself is thus here the source of time and is time itself. Therefore time is not to be determined by analogy nor by any other means, but it is necessary to maintain *Enargie* itself, for sense perception reflected in itself is time itself, there is no way of going beyond it.

On the other hand, in Lucretius, Sextus Empiricus and Stobaeus [2] accidents of accidents, change reflected in itself, is determined as time. The reflection of the accidents in sense perception and their reflection in itself are therefore posited as one and the same.

[1] Diogen. Laert. X, 72. There is another thing which we must consider carefully. We must not investigate time as we do the other accidents which we investigate in a subject, namely, by referring them to the preconceptions envisioned in our minds; but we must take into account the plain fact itself, in virtue of which we speak of time as long or short, linking to it in intimate connexion this attribute of duration. We need not adopt any fresh terms as preferable, but should employ the usual expressions about it. Nor need we predicate anything else of time, as if this something else contained the same essence as is contained in the proper meaning of the word "time" (for this also is done by some). We must chiefly reflect upon that to which we attach this peculiar character of time, and by which we measure it. No further proof is required: we have only to reflect that we attach the attribute of time to days and nights and their parts, and likewise to feelings of pleasure and pain and to neutral states, to states of movement and states of rest, conceiving a peculiar accident of these to be this very characteristic which we expressed by the word "time." (He says this both in the second book "On Nature" and in the Larger Epitome).

[2] Lucret. De Rer. Nat. l.c. Sext. Empir. adv. Math.

By means of this connection between time and sensibility the *eidōla*, which are also found in Democritus, acquire a more consistent status. The *eidōla* are the forms of natural bodies which peel off from them as it were as surfaces and cause them to enter into appearance.[1] These forms of things constantly flow from them and press against the senses and in just this way allow objects to appear. Therefore, in hearing nature hears itself, in smelling it smells itself, in seeing it sees itself.[2] Human sensibility is thus the medium in which, as in a focus, natural processes reflect themselves and ignite themselves to become the light of appearance.

In Democritus this is an inconsistency since appearance is only subjective; in Epicurus it is a necessary conclusion since sensibility is the reflection of the appearing world in itself, its embodied time.

Finally, the relation of sensibility and time exhibits itself in such a way that the temporality of things and their appearance to the senses are posited as intrinsically one. It is precisely because bodies appear to the sense that they pass away.[3] Indeed, the *eidōla*, by perpetually separating themselves from the bodies and flowing into the senses, by having their sensibility outside themselves as another nature, by not returning into themselves, i.e. not out of the diremption – for these reasons they dissolve and perish.

[1] Diogen. Laert. X, 46.
Lucret. IV, 30 sqq.

.... images of things ......
which, like films drawn from the outermost surface
of things, flit about hither and thither in the air.

Id. IV, 52 sqq.

Semblances and their shapes of things are
thrown off from their outer surface ....
like the body from which it is shed to go
on its way.

[2] Diogen. Laert. X, 49. We must also consider that it is by the entrance of something coming from external objects that we see their shapes and think of them. For external things would not stamp on us their own nature of colour and form through the medium of the air which is between them and us ... These films or outlines coming from the things themselves being of the same colour and shape as the external things themselves. They move with rapid motion; and this again explains why they present the appearance of the single continuous object, and retain the mutual interconnexion which they had in the object when they impinge upon the senses ... Again, hearing takes place when a current passes from the object, whether person or thing, which emits voice or sound or noise, or produces the sensation of hearing in any way whatever. This current is broken up into homogeneous particles, which at the same time preserve a certain mutual connexion and a distinctive unity extending to the object which emitted them. ... Again, we must believe that smelling, like hearing, would produce no sensation, were there not particles conveyed from the object which are of the proper sort for exciting the organ of smelling ...

[3] Lucret. de Rer. Nat. II, 1145.

With good reason therefore the things pass away,
since by the flowing off they have become thinned.

Thus as the atom is nothing but the natural form of the abstract, individual self-consciousness, so sensible nature is only the objectivity of the empirical, individual self-consciousness, and this is what constitutes sensibility. The senses are therefore the only criteria in concrete nature, as abstract reason is the only criterion in the world of atoms.

V. The Meteors

Democritus' astronomical views may be considered sagacious from the point of view of their time. But they are of no philosophical interest. They do not rise above the sphere of empirical reflection nor are they in any definite way related to the doctrine of atoms.

By contrast, Epicurus' theory of the heavenly bodies and the processes connected to them or the meteors (the single expression includes both) stands in contrast not only to Democritus' opinion but to the opinion of Greek philosophy in general. The adoration of the heavenly bodies is a cult which all Greek philosophers celebrate. The system of the heavenly bodies is the first kind of naive and naturally determined existence of true reason. Greek self-consciousness has the same position in the realm of the mind. It is the intellectual solar system. Greek philosophy thus worshipped its own mind in the heavenly bodies.

Anaxagoras, who was the first to give a physical explanation of the heavens and thus drew them down to earth, but in another sense than Socrates, answered in this way when asked why he had been born: *eis theōrian hēliou kai selēnēs kai ouranou.*[1] Xenophanes however looked at the heavens and said: The one is God.[2] The religious affinity for the heavenly bodies is well known in the Pythagoreans, Plato and Aristotle.

Indeed, Epicurus opposed the view of the whole Greek people.

It seems sometimes, says Aristotle, that the concept bears testimony to the phenomenon, and sometimes the phenomena to the concept. Thus all men have an idea of gods and ascribe the highest place to them, the barbarians as well as the Hellenes. As many as believe in the existence of the gods clearly connect the immortal with the immortal, because the contrary is impossible. Thus if there exists a divinity, as there really does, then our statement about the substance of the heavenly bodies is also correct. But this also corresponds to the sensible perception and human conviction is justified. In all of the past there seems to have been, according to mutually handed-down recollection, no

[1] Diogen. Laert. II, 3.10.
[2] Aristot. Metaphys. I, 5.

change either in the whole heavens or in any of its parts. Even the name seems to be traditional from the ancients down to our own time, in that they assumed the same things that we also say. Not once, not twice, but an infinite number of times the same views have come down to us. Indeed, because the first body is something other than earth, fire, air, or water, they called the highest place "Ether" from *thein aei*, giving it the epithet: eternal time.[1] But the ancients assigned the heavens and the highest place to the gods because they alone are immortal. The current doctrine proves, however, that it is indestructible, uncreated, non-participating in any mortal misfortune. In this way our concepts correspond likewise to the prophecy about God.[2] That there is one heaven is clear. It is a tradition from our ancestors and the ancients, having remained in the form of myth in subsequent generations, that the heavenly bodies are gods and that the divine encompasses all of nature. The other idea was mythically added for the belief of the masses, as useful for law and life. For they make the gods similar to men and to some of the other living creatures, and invent other things of this kind connected and related to it. If we make a distinction here and only fasten on the first idea their belief that the first substances are gods – then we must regard it as divinely given and we must hold that afterwards, as it happened, every possible art and philosophy was invented and lost again, and these opinions, like relics, have come down to the present world.[3]

Epicurus, on the contrary, said: To all this there is to be added the thought that the greatest confusion of the human soul arises in that people consider the heavenly bodies blissful and indestructible, and they have wishes and actions opposed to them, and become suspicious

[1] Aristot. de Caelo. I, 3. I think too that the argument bears out experience and is borne out by it. All men have a conception of gods, and all assign the highest place to the divine, both barbarians and Hellenes, as many as believe in gods, supposing, obviously, that immortality is closely linked with the immortal. It could not, they think, be otherwise. If then – and it is true – there is something divine, what we have said about the primary bodily substance is well said. The truth of it is also clear from the evidence of the senses, enough at least to warrant the assent of human faith; for throughout all past time, according to the records handed down from generation to generation, we find no trace of change either in the whole of the outermost heaven or in any one of its proper parts. It seems too that the name of this first body has been passed down to the present time by the ancients, who thought of it in the same way as we do, for we cannot help believing that the same ideas recur to men not once nor twice but over and over again. Thus they, believing that the primary body was something different from earth and fire and air and water, gave the name aither to the uppermost region, choosing its title from the fact that it "runs always" and eternally.

[2] Ib.id. II, 1. Our forefathers assigned heaven, the upper region, to the gods, in the belief that it alone was imperishable . . . it is the only way in which we can give a consistent account and one which fits in with our premonitions of divinity.

[3] Aristot. Metaphys. XI, 8.

of the myths.[1] So far as the meteors are concerned, one must believe that motion and position and eclipse and rising and setting and things related to these do not originate in them, since One rules and orders or has ordered, who at the same time possesses all bliss and indestructibility. Actions do not agree with bliss, rather actions occur in a way closely related to weakness, fear and need. It is no longer believed that some fire-like bodies, possessing bliss, willingly submit themselves to these motions. If one does not agree with this, then this contrast itself produces the greatest confusion for souls.[2]

If Aristotle reproaches the ancients for believing that the heavens require the support of Atlas,[3] the

pros hesperous topous
hesteke kion ouranou te kai chthonos
omion ereidon

(Aeschyl. Prometh. 348 sq.)

Epicurus on the other hand criticizes those who believe that man needs the heavens, and Atlas himself, upon whom the heavens are supported, he finds to possess human stupidity and superstition. Stupidity and superstition are also Titans.

Except for the last section, the whole letter of Epicurus to Pythocles has to do with the theory of the heavenly bodies. The last section closes the epistle with ethical aphorisms. And ethical maxims are suitably appended to the theory of the meteors. This theory is a matter of conscience for Epicurus. Our consideration will, therefore, base itself mainly on this letter to Phythocles. We will supplement it with the letter to Herodotus, to whom Epicurus refers in his letter to Pythocles.[4]

First, it is not necessary to believe that from knowledge of the meteors, let them be comprehended as a whole or in detail, any other goal can be reached than *ataraxis* and firm confidence, as with the rest

[1] Diogen. Laert. X, 81. There is yet one more point to seize, namely, that the greatest anxiety of the human mind arises through the belief that the heavenly bodies are blessed and indestructible, and that at the same time they have volitions, and actions and causality inconsistent with this belief ... expecting evil because of the myths.

[2] Id. ib. 76. Nay more: we are bound to believe that in the sky revolutions, solstices, eclipses, rising and settings, and the like, take place without the ministration or command, either now or in the future, of any being who at the same time enjoys perfect bliss along with immortality. For troubles and anxieties ... do not accord with bliss, but always imply weakness and fear and dependence upon one's neighbors ... Such inconsistency will of itself suffice to produce the worst disturbance in our minds.

[3] Aristot. de Caelo. II, 1. There is no need, therefore, in the first place to give credence to the ancient mythological explanation according to which it owes its safety to an Atlas.

[4] Diogen. Laert. X, 85. (To Pythocles) So you will do well to take and learn them and get them up quickly along with the short epitome in my letter to Herodotus.

of natural science.[1] Our life does not need ideologies and empty hypotheses, but that we live without confusion. As it is the business of physiology in general to investigate the reasons for primary things, so it is that knowledge of the meteors brings happiness. In and of itself the theory of setting and rising, of position and situation, contains no particular reason for happiness; only that error possesses those who see these simple phenomena without understanding their nature and their main causes.[2] The only theory which has been denied up to this point is the pre-eminence which the theory of the meteors is supposed to have over the other sciences, and this theory is placed on the same level as the others.

But the theory of the meteors differs more specifically from the ethical method as well as from other physical problems, for example, from the affirmation that there are indivisible elements and the like where only a single explanation corresponds to the phenomenon. For this does not happen with the meteors.[3] They have no simple cause of origin and have more than one category of being wich corresponds to the phenomenon. Physiology is not to be carried on according to empty axioms and laws.[4] It is constantly repeated that the meteors are not to be explained *haplos* (simply, absolutely), but *pollachos* (in many ways). This applies to the rising and setting of the sun and moon,[5] to the wax-

[1] Id. ib. 85. In the first place, remember that, like everything else, knowledge of celestial phenomena, whether taken along with other things or in isolation, has no other end in view than peace of mind and firm conviction.

Id. ib. 82. But mental tranquillity means being released from all these troubles and cherishing a continual remembrance of the highest and most important truths.

[2] Id. ib. 87. For our life has no need now of unreason and false opinion; our one need is untroubled existence.

Ib. 78. Further, we must hold that to arrive at accurate knowledge of the causes of things of most moment is the business of natural science, and that happiness depends on this (viz. on the knowledge of celestial and atmospheric phenomena).

Ib. 79. But when we come to subjects for special inquiry,there is nothing in the knowledge of risings and settings and solstices and eclipses and all kindred subjects that contribute to our happiness, but those who are well-informed about such matters and yet are ignorant as to what the heavenly bodies really are, and what are the most important causes of phenomena, feel quite as much fear as those who have no such special information.

[3] Id. ib. 86. We do not seek to wrest by force what is impossible, nor to understand all matters equally well, nor make our treatment always as clear as when we discuss human life or explain the principles of physics in general – for instance, that the whole of being consists of bodies and intangible nature, or any other proposition which admits only one explanation of the phenomena to be possible. But this is not the case with celestial phenomena. These at any rate admit of manifold causes for their occurrence.

[4] Id. ib. 86. Celestial phenomena admit of manifold accounts, none of them contradictory of sensation, of their nature. For in the study of nature we must not conform to empty assumptions and arbitrary laws, but follow the promptings of the facts.

[5] Id. ib. 92.

ing and waning of the moon,[1] to the illusion of the face in the moon,[2] to the change of the length of day and night [3] and all celestial phenomena.

Now how is this to be explained?

Any explanation is sufficient. Only let myth be avoided. It will be be avoided if, following the phenomena, one draws conclusions from them concerning the obscure.[4] One must hold fast to appearance, to sense perception. The analogy is, therefore, applicable. One can thus explain away fear and free one's self from it, giving reasons concerning the meteors and the other things that always happen and dismay the rest of mankind.[5]

The mass of explanations, the multiplicity of possibilities should not only calm consciousness and remove reasons for fear, but should at the same time deny unity, the absolute law which is always the same in the heavenly bodies. The situation could be this way, it could be some other way; this lawless possibility is the character of their reality, everything in them is impermanent and unstable.[6] The multiplicity of explanations should at the same time remove the unity of the object.

While Aristotle in agreement with the other Greek philosophers makes the heavenly bodies eternal and immortal because they always behave in the same way, while he ascribes to them their own, higher

[1] Id. ib. 94.

[2] Id. ib. 95 and 96.

[3] Id. ib. 98.

[4] Id. ib. 104. Exclusion of myth is the sole condition necessary, and it will be excluded, if one properly attends to the facts and hence draws inferences to interpret what is obscure.

[5] Id. ib. 80. We must not suppose that our treatment of these matters fails of accuracy, so far as it is needful to ensure our tranquillity and happiness.

Ib. 82. Mental tranquillity means being released from all these troubles. Hence we must attend to present feelings and sense perceptions, whether those of mankind in general or those peculiar to the individual, and also attend to all the clear evidence available, as given by each of the standards of truth. For by studying them we shall rightly trace to its cause and banish the source of disturbance and dread, accounting for celestian phenomena and for all the things which from time to time befall us and cause the utmost alarm to the rest of mankind.

Ib. 87. Some phenomena within our experience afford evidence by which we may interpret what goes on in the heavens. We see how the former really take place, but not how the celestial phenomena take place, for this occurrence may possibly be due to a variety of causes. However, we must observe each fact as presented, and further separate from it all the facts presented along with it, the occurrence of which from various causes is not contradicted by facts within our experience.

[6] Id. ib. 78. We must recognize in such points as this no plurality of causes or contingency, but must hold that nothing suggestive of conflict or disquiet is compatible with an immortal and blessed nature.

Id. ib. 86. These at any rate admit of manifold causes for their occurrence.

Id. ib. 87. All things go on interruptedly, if all be explained by the method of plurality of causes in conformity with the facts ... But when we pick and choose among them we clearly fall away from the study of nature altogether.

element not subjected to the force of gravity, Epicurus in direct contrast makes the claim that it is exactly the other way around. By virtue of this his theory of the meteors is specifically different from all other physical theory, that everything happens in them multitudinously and ungoverned, that everything in them is to be explained by numerous and inexact, large numbers of reasons. Indeed, angry and violently declaiming, he rejects the opposite opinion which holds itself to one method of explanation and excludes all others, which assumes something unified, therefore, eternal and divine in the meteors, which has fallen into vain explanation and the slavish tricks of the astrologers. Epicurus claims that those of the opposite opinion overstep the bounds of physiology and throw themselves into the arms of myth, attempt to achieve the impossible and devote great effort to nonsense. They do not even know, he affirms, where *ataraxy* gets into difficulty. Epicurus holds their chatter in contempt.[1] We must avoid the prejudice that the investigation of these objects is not thorough and subtle enough, since it has as a goal only our *ataraxy* and happiness.[2] On the contrary it is an absolute norm that nothing can be ascribed to an indestructible and eternal nature that destroys *ataraxy*, which produces danger. Consciousness must understand that this is an absolute law.[3]

[1] Id. ib. 98. Those who adopt only one explanation are in conflict with the facts and are utterly mistaken as to the way in which man can attain knowledge.

Ib. 113. To assign a single cause for these effects when the facts suggest several causes is madness and a strange inconsistency; yet it is done by adherents of rash astronomy, who assign meaningless causes for the stars whenever they persist in saddling the divinity with burdensome tasks.

Ib. 97. And further, let the regularity of their orbits be explained in the same way as certain ordinary incidents within our own experience; the divine nature must not on any account be adduced to explain this, but must be kept free from the task and in perfect bliss. Unless this be done, the whole study of celestial phenomena will be in vain, as indeed it has proved to be with some who did not lay hold of a possible method, but fell into the folly of supposing that these events happen in one single way only and of rejecting all the others which are possible, suffering themselves to be carried into the realm of the unintelligible, and being unable to take a comprehensive view of the facts which must be taken as clues to the rest.

Ib. 93. We should be unmoved by the servile artifices of the astronomers.

Ib. 87. When we pick and choose among causes we clearly fall away from the study of nature altogether and tumble into myth.

Ib. 80. When therefore we investigate the causes of celestial and atmospheric phenomena, as of all that is unknown, we must take into account the variety of ways in which analogous occurrences happen within our experience; while as for those who do not recognize the differences between what is or comes about from a single cause and that which may be the effect of any one of several causes, overlooking the fact that the objects are only seen at a distance, and are moreover ignorant of the conditions that render, or do not render, peace of mind impossible.

[2] Id. ib. 80. We must not suppose that our treatment of these matters fails of accuracy so far as it is needful to ensure our tranquillity and happiness.

[3] Id. ib. 78. Nothing suggestive of conflict or disquiet is compatible with an immortal and blessed nature. And the mind can grasp the absolute truth of this.

Thus Epicures concludes: Because the eternity of the heavenly bodies would disturb the ataraxia of self-consciousness, it is a necessary, stringent conclusion that the heavenly bodies are not eternal.

Now how is this peculiar view of Epicurus to be understood?

All authors who have written about Epicurean philosophy have presented this theory as incongruous with the rest of his physics, with the atomic theory. The battle against the Stoics, superstition and astrology are given by these authors as sufficient reasons for the theory.

We have heard that Epicurus himself differentiates the method which is applied in his theory of meteors from the method in the rest of his physics. But in what determination of his principle element does the necessity of his differentiation lie? How does he come across this idea?

He fights not only against astrology but against astronomy itself, against eternal law and reason in explaining the heavenly system. In the last analysis his opposition to the Stoics explains nothing. Their superstition and their whole view were already refuted by the fact that the celestial bodies were spoken of as accidental complexes of atoms and their processes as the accidental motion of these atoms. Their eternal nature was annihilated by this – a conclusion which Democritus was satisfied to draw from that premise.[1] Indeed, their very existence had been disposed of.[2] Atomistics consequently needed no new method.

This is still not the whole difficulty. An even more enigmatic antinomy arises.

The atom is matter in the form of autonomy, of individuality, as it were, the representation of weight. But, the heavenly bodies are the highest reality of weight. In them all antinomies between form and matter, between concept and existence, which form the development of the atom are solved, in them all determinations which are demanded are realized. The celestial bodies are eternal and unchanging; they have their center of gravity in themselves, not outside themselves. Their only action is motion, and separated by empty space, they deviate from the straight line, form a system of repulsion and attraction in which they maintain all their autonomy and finally engender time out of themselves as the form of their appearance. Thus the heavenly bodies are atoms become real. In them matter has received individuality. Here Epicurus must have seen the highest existence of his principle element, the peak and finale of his system. He alleged that he created the atoms

[1] Cf. Aristot. de Caelo I. 10.

[2] Id. ib. I, 10. If then the world has been formed out of elements which once were otherwise than they are now, if they had always been in that state and it was impossible for them to change, it could never have come into being at all.

so that immortal foundations would lie at the basis of nature. He alleged that he was concerned about the substantial individuality of matter. But, where he finds the reality of his nature – because he knows no other than the mechanical – in autonomous, indestructible matter, in the heavenly bodies, whose eternality an immutability are proven by the belief of the people, the judgment of philosophy, the evidence of the senses – there it is his single effort to draw them back down into earthly transitoriness. It is at this point that he turns zealously against the worshippers of autonomous nature which contains the point of individuality within itself. This is his greatest contradiction.

Therefore, Epicurus feels that his earlier categories go to pieces here, that the method of his theory becomes a different one. And, this is the deepest wisdom of his system, the most thorough consistency, that he feels this and expresses it consciously.

We have seen how the whole Epicurean philosophy of nature is flooded with the contradiction between essence and existence, between form and matter. But in the heavenly bodies this contradiction is erased, the conflicting elements are reconciled. In the celestial system matter has received form within itself, has taken into itself individuality and thus achieved autonomy.But at this point it stops being affirmation of the abstract self-consciousness. In the world of atoms as in the world of appearance, form battled with matter; one determination destroyed the other, and precisely in this contradiction the abstract, individual self-consciousness senses its nature objectified. The abstract form which battled with abstract matter under the form of matter was matter itself. But now, where matter has reconciled itself with form and is objectified, the individual self-consciousness steps out of its husk, announces itself as the true principle element and contends against nature which has become autonomous.

From another point of view it can be expressed in this way: matter, by receiving individuality within itself, for, as is the case with celestial bodies, has ceased to be an abstract individual. It has become concrete individuality, generality. Thus in the meteors the abstract, individual self-consciousness is confronted with its objective refutation – the general attains existence and nature. Therefore, it recognizes in them its mortal enemy. Thus it attributes to them, as Epicurus does, all the fear and confusion of human beings, because the fear and dissolution of the abstract individual is the general. So here the true principle element of Epicurus, the abstract, individual self-consciousness, is concealed no longer. It steps out from its hiding place and, freed from material disguise, it seeks to destroy the reality of autonomous nature in terms of abstract possibility – what is possible can also be different; the opposite of the possible is also possible. From this comes the polemic against those who explain the heavenly bodies *haplos*, i.e. in a certain way, that the One is necessary and autonomous in itself.

Thus as long as nature as atom and appearance expresses the individual self-consciousness and its contradiction, the subjectivity of the latter appears only in the form of matter itself; where, on the other hand, it becomes autonomous, it is reflected in itself and opposes nature in its own shape as autonomous form.

It should have been said from the beginning that when Epicurus' principle element is realized it will stop having any reality for him. If the individual self-consciousness had been placed in reality under the determination of nature or nature under its determination, then its determination, i.e. its existence would have ceased, because only the general in free differentiation from itself can know at the same time its affirmation.

In the theory of meteors, therefore, the soul of the Epicurean philosophy of nature appears. Nothing is eternal which annihilates the *ataraxy* of the individual self-consciousness. The heavenly bodies disturb its *ataraxy*, its identity with itself, because they are existing generality, because nature has become autonomous in them. Thus it is not the belly-doctrine of Archestratus, as Chrysippus thinks,[1] but the absolute character and freedom of self-consciousness which is the principle element of Epicurean philosophy, even if self-consciousness is only conceived in the form of individuality.

If the abstract, individual self-consciousness is posited as an absolute principle element, then certainly all true and real science is destroyed insofar as individuality does not rule in the nature of things themselves. But then, too, everything collapses which behaves transcendentally over and against human consciousness, i.e. belongs to the imaginative intellect. On the other hand, if self-consciousness, which only knows itself under the form of abstract generality, is made to become an absolute principle element, then the door is opened wide to superstitions and servile mysticism. The historical proof of this can be found in Stoic philosophy. The abstract, general self-consciousness has the urge to affirm itself in things in which it is only affirmed by denying them.

1

Epicurus is, therefore, the greatest Greek representative of the Enlightenment, and he deserves the praise of Lucretius[1]:

when man's life lay for all to see foully grovelling upon the ground, crushed beneath the weight of Religion, which displayed her head in the regions of heaven, threatening mortals from on high with horrible aspect, a man of Greece was the first that dared to uplift mortal eyes against her, the first to make stand against her; for neither bables of the gods could quell him, nor thunderbolts, nor heaven with menacing roar, nay all the more, they goaded the eager courage of his soul, so that he should desire, first of all men, to shatter the confining bars of nature's gates. Therefore the lively power of his mind prevailed, and forth he marched far beyond the flaming walls of the heavens, as he traversed the immeasurable universe in thought and imagination; whence victorious he returns bearing his prize, the knowledge what can come into being, what can not, in a word, how each thing has its powers defined and its deep-set boundary mark. Wherefore Religion is now in her turn cast down and trampled underfoot, whilst we by the victory are exalted high as heaven.

The difference between the Democritean and Epicurean philosophy of nature which we established at the end of the general section, has been confirmed and developed in all spheres of nature. In Epicurus, therefore, the atomistic theory with all its contradictions is carried through and perfected as the natural science of self-consciousness to its highest conclusion which is as an absolute principle in the form of abstract individuality – its dissolution and conscious opposition against the universal. For Democritus, in contrast, the atom is only the general, objective expression of empirical investigation of nature in general. The atom remains for him a pure and abstract category, a hypothesis, which is the result of experience, not its energizing principle element, which remains without realization just as the real investigation of nature is no further affected by it.

1